# Ted Hughes

# MOORTOWN

**Drawings by Leonard Baskin**

**HARPER COLOPHON BOOKS**
Harper & Row, Publishers
New York, Cambridge, Philadelphia, San Francisco
London, Mexico City, São Paulo, Sydney

## Also by Ted Hughes

### Poetry

REMAINS OF ELMET • CAVE BIRDS • SEASON SONGS
GAUDETE • SELECTED POEMS (1957-1967) • CROW
WODWO • LUPERCAL
THE HAWK IN THE RAIN

### Drama

SENECA'S OEDIPUS (adaptation) • ORGHAST

### Prose

POETRY IS

### For Children

(edited)  WITH FAIREST FLOWERS WHILE SUMMER LASTS:
Verse from Shakespeare
THE IRON GIANT • HOW THE WHALE BECAME

"Bride and Groom Lie Hidden for Three Days" first appeared in *Cave Birds: An Alchemical Cave Drama* published by The Viking Press.

A hardcover edition of this book is published by Harper & Row, Publishers, Inc.

First HARPER COLOPHON edition published 1983.

Library of Congress Cataloging in Publication Data

Hughes, Ted, 1930-
    Moortown.

    I. Title.
PR6058.U37M68 1980     821'.914     79-3396
ISBN 0-06-091017-8 (pbk.)   83 84 85 86 10 9 8 7 6 5 4 3 2 1

# Contents

MOORTOWN

## PROMETHEUS ON HIS CRAG

iv

## EARTH–NUMB

## ADAM AND THE
## SACRED NINE

# MOORTOWN

# Rain

Rain. Floods. Frost. And after frost, rain.
Dull roof-drumming. Wraith-rain pulsing across purple-bare
woods
Like light across heaved water. Sleet in it.
And the poor fields, miserable tents of their hedges.
Mist-rain off-world. Hills wallowing
In and out of a gray or silvery dissolution. A farm gleaming,
Then all dull in the near drumming. At field corners
Brown water backing and brimming in grass.
Toads hop across rain-hammered roads. Every mutilated leaf
there
Looks like a frog or a rained-out mouse. Cattle
Wait under blackened backs. We drive post holes.
They half fill with water before the post goes in.
Mud-water spurts as the iron bar slam-burns
The oak stakehead dry. Cows
Tamed on the waste mudded like a rugby field
Stand and watch, come very close for company
In the rain that goes on and on, and gets colder.
They sniff the wire, sniff the tractor, watch. The hedges
Are straggles of gap. A few haws. Every half-ton cow
Sinks to the fetlock at every sliding stride.
They are ruining their field and they know it.
They look out sideways from under their brows which are
Their only shelter. The sunk scrubby wood
Is a pulverized wreck, rain riddles its holes
To the drowned roots. A pheasant looking black
In his waterproofs bends at his job in the stubble.

The midafternoon dusk soaks into
The soaked thickets. Nothing protects them.
The fox corpses lie beaten to their bare bones,
Skin beaten off, brains and bowels beaten out.
Nothing but their blueprint bones lasts in the rain,
Sodden soft. Round their hay racks, calves
Stand in a shine of mud. The gateways
Are deep obstacles of mud. The calves look up, through
                                    plastered forelocks,
Without moving. Nowhere they can go
Is less uncomfortable. The brimming world
And the pouring sky are the only places
For them to be. Fieldfares squeal over, sodden
Toward the sodden wood. A raven,
Cursing monotonously, goes over fast
And vanishes in rain-mist. Magpies
Shake themselves hopelessly, hop in the spatter. Misery.
Surviving green of ferns and brambles is tumbled
Like an abandoned scrapyard. The calves
Wait deep beneath their spines. Cows roar
Then hang their noses to the mud.
Snipe go over, invisible in the dusk,
With their squelching cries.

# Dehorning

Bad-tempered bullying bunch, the horned cows
Among the unhorned. Feared, spoilt.
Cantankerous at the hay, at assemblies, at crowded
Yard operations. Knowing their horntips' position
To a fraction, every other cow knowing it too,
Like their own tenderness. Horning of bellies, hair-tufting
Of horntips. Handy levers. But
Off with the horns.
So there they all are in the yard—
The pick of the bullies, churning each other
Like thick fish in a bucket, churning their mud.
One by one, into the cage of the crush: the needle,
A roar not like a cow—more like a tiger,
Blast of air down a cavern, and long, long,
Beginning in pain and ending in terror—then the next.
The needle between the horn and the eye, so deep
Your gut squirms for the eyeball twisting
In its pink-white fastenings of tissue. This side and that.
Then the first one anesthetized, back in the crush.
The bulldog pincers in the septum, stretched full strength,
The horn levered right over, the chin pulled round
With the pincers, the mouth drooling, the eye
Like a live eye caught in a pan, like the eye of a fish
Imprisoned in air. Then the cheese cutter
Of braided wire, and stainless-steel peg handles,
Aligned on the hair-bedded root of the horn, then leaning
Backward full weight, pull-punching backwards,
Left right left right and the blood leaks

Down over the cheekbone, the wire bites
And buzzes, the ammonia horn-burn smokes
And the cow groans, roars shapelessly, hurls
Its half-ton commotion in the tight cage. Our faces
Grimace like faces in the dentist's chair. The horn
Rocks from its roots, the wire pulls through
The last hinge of hair, the horn is heavy and free,
And a water-pistol jet of blood
Rains over the one who holds it—a needle jet
From the white-rasped and bloody skull crater. Then tweezers
Twiddle the artery nozzle, knotting it enough,
And purple antiseptic squirts a cuttlefish cloud over it.
Then the other side the same. We collect
A heap of horns. The floor of the crush
Is a trampled puddle of scarlet. The purple-crowned cattle,
The bullies, with suddenly no horns to fear,
Start ramming and wrestling. Maybe their heads
Are still anesthetized. A new order
Among the hornless. The bitchy high-headed
Straight-back brindle, with her Spanish bull trot,
And her head-shaking snorting advance and her crazy spirit,
Will have to get maternal. What she's lost
In weapons, she'll have to make up for in tits.
But they've all lost one third of their beauty.

# Poor Birds

In the boggy copse. Blue
Dusk presses into their skulls
Electrodes of stars. All night
Clinging to sodden twigs, with twiggy claws,
They dream the featherless, ravenous
Machinery of heaven. At dawn, fevered,
They flee to the field. All day
They try to get some proper sleep without
Losing sight of the grass. Panics
Fling them from hill to hill. They search everywhere
For the safety that sleeps
Everywhere in the closed faces
Of stones.

# Struggle

We had been expecting her to calve
And there she was, just after dawn, down.
Private, behind bushed hedge cuttings, in a low rough corner.
The walk towards her was like a walk into danger.
Caught by her first calf, the small-boned black and white
                                        heifer
Having a bad time. She lifted her head,
She reached for us with a wild, flinging look
And flopped flat again.
There was the calf,
White-faced, lion-colored, enormous, trapped
Round the waist by his mother's purpled elastic,
His heavy long forelegs limply bent in a not-yet-inherited
                                        gallop,
His head curving up and back, pushing for the udder
Which had not yet appeared, his nose scratched and reddened
By an ill-placed clump of bitten-off rushes,
His fur dried as if he had been
Half born for hours, as he probably had.
Then we heaved on his forelegs,
And on his neck, and half born he mooed,
Protesting about everything. Then bending him down,
Between her legs, and sliding a hand
Into the hot tunnel, trying to ease
His sharp hipbones past her pelvis,
Then twisting him down, so you expected
His spine to slip its sockets,
And one hauling his legs, and one embracing his wet waist

Like pulling somebody anyhow from a bog,
And one with hands easing his hips past the corners
Of his tunnel mother, till something gave.
The cow flung her head and lifted her upper hind leg
With every heave, and something gave
Almost a click—
And his scrubbed wet enormous flanks came sliding out,
Colored ready for the light his incredibly long hind legs
From the loose red flapping sack mouth
Followed by a gush of colors, a mess
Of puddled tissues and jellies.
He mooed feebly and lay like a pietà Christ
In the cold easterly daylight. We dragged him
Under his mother's nose, her stretched-out exhausted head,
So she could get to know him with lickings.
They lay face to face like two mortally wounded duelists.
We stood back, letting the strength flow towards them.
We gave her a drink, we gave her hay. The calf
Started his convalescence
From the grueling journey. All day he lay
Overpowered by limpness and weight.
We poured his mother's milk into him
But he had not strength to swallow.
He made a few clumsy throat gulps, then lay
Mastering just breathing.
We took him inside. We tucked him up
In front of a stove, and tried to pour
Warm milk and whisky down his throat and not into his lungs.

But his eye just lay suffering the monstrous weight of his head,
The impossible job of his marvelous huge limbs.
He could not make it. He died called Struggle.
Son of Patience.

# Feeding Out-Wintering Cattle
## at Twilight

The wind is inside the hill.
The wood is a struggle—like a wood
Struggling through a wood. A panic
Only just holds off—every gust
Breaches the sky walls and it seems, this time,
The whole sea of air will pour through,
The thunder will take deep hold, roots
Will have to come out, every loose thing
Will have to lift and go. And the cows, dark lumps of dusk,
Stand waiting, like nails in a tin roof,
For the crucial moment, taking the strain
In their stirring stillness. As if their hooves
Held their field in place, held the hill
To its trembling shape. Night-thickness
Purples in the turmoil, making
Everything more alarming. Unidentifiable, tiny
Birds go past like elf bolts.
Battling the hay bales from me, the cows
Jostle and crush, like hulls blown from their moorings
And piling at the jetty. The wind
Has got inside their wintry buffalo skins,
Their wild woolly bulk-heads, their fierce, joyful breathings
And the reckless strength of their necks.
What do they care their hooves
Are knee-deep in porage of earth—
The hay blows luminous tatters from their chewings,
A fiery loss, frittering downwind,

Snatched away over the near edge
Where the world becomes water
Thundering like a flood river at night.
They grunt happily, half dissolved
On their steep, hurtling brink, as I flounder back
Towards headlights.

# Fox Hunt

Two days after Xmas, near noon, as I listen
The hounds behind the hill
Are changing ground, a cloud of excitements,
Their voices like rusty, reluctant
Rolling stock being shunted. The hunt
Has tripped over a fox
At the threshold of the village. A crow in the fir
Is inspecting his nesting site, and he expostulates
At the indecent din. A blackbird
Starts up its cat-alarm. The gray-cloud mugginess
Of the year in its pit trying to muster
Enough energy to start opening again
Roars distantly. Everything sodden. The fox
Is flying, taking his first lesson
From the idiot pack-noise, the puppyish whine-yelps
Curling up like hounds' tails, and the gruff military barkers:
A machine with only two products—
Dog shit and dead foxes. Lorry engines
As usual modulating on the main street hill
Complicate the air, and the fox runs in a suburb
Of indifferent civilized noises. Now the yelpings
Enrich their brocade, thickening closer
In the maze of wind currents. The orchards
And the hedges stand in coma. The pastures
Have got off so far lightly, are firm, cattle
Still nose hopefully, as if spring might be here
Missing out winter. Big lambs
Are organizing their gangs in gateways. The fox

13

Hangs his silver tongue in the world of noise
Over his spattering paws. Will he run
Till his muscles suddenly turn to iron,
Till blood froths his mouth as his lungs tatter,
Till his feet are raw blood-sticks and his tail
Trails thin as a rat's? Or will he
Make a mistake, jump the wrong way, jump right
Into the hound's mouth? As I write this down
He runs still fresh, with all his chances before him.

# New Year Exhilaration

On the third day
Finds its proper weather. Pressure
Climbing and the hard blue sky
Scoured by gales. The world's being
Swept clean. Twigs that can't cling
Go flying, last leaves ripped off
Bowl along roads like daring mice. Imagine
The new moon high tide sea under this
Rolling of air weights. Exhilaration
Lashes everything. Windows flash,
White houses dazzle, fields glow red.
Seas pour in over the land, invisible maelstroms
Set the house joints creaking. Every twig end
Writes its circles and the earth
Is massaged with roots. The powers of hills
Hold their bright faces in the wind shine.
The hills are being honed. The river
Thunders like a factory, its weirs
Are tremendous engines. People
Walk precariously, the whole landscape
Is imperiled, like a tarpaulin
With the wind under it. "It nearly
Blew me up the chimbley!" And a laugh
Blows away like a hat.

# Snow Smoking as the Fields Boil

The bull weeps.
The trough solidifies.
The cock pheasant has forgotten his daughters.
The fox crosses midfield, careless of acquittal.
Twigs cannot pay the interest.
The farm roofs sink in the welter again, like a whale's fluke.
Sheep fade humbly.
The owl cries early, breaking parole,
With icicles darkening witness.

# Bringing in New Couples

Wind out of freezing Europe. A mean snow
Fiery cold. Ewes caked crusty with snow,
Their new hot lambs wet trembling
And crying on trampled patches, under the hedge—
Twenty miles of open lower landscape
Blows into their wetness. The field smokes and writhes,
Burning like a moor with snow fumes.
Lambs nestling to make themselves comfortable
While the ewe nudges and nibbles at them
And the numbing snow wind blows on the blood tatters
At her breached back end.
The moor a gray sea shape. The wood
Thick-fingered density, a worked wall of whiteness.
The old sea-roar, sheep-shout, lamb-wail.
Redwings needling invisible. A fright
Smoking among trees, the hedges blocked.
Lifting of ice-heavy ewes, trampling anxieties
As they follow their wide-legged tall lambs,
Tripods craning to cry bewildered.
We coax the mothers to follow their babies
And they do follow, running back
In sudden convinced panic to the patch
Where the lamb had been born, dreading
She must have been deceived away from it
By crafty wolvish humans, then coming again
Defenseless to the bleat she's attuned to
And recognizing her own—a familiar
Detail in the meaningless shape mass

Of human arms, legs, body-clothes—her lamb on the white
earth
Held by those hands. Then vanishing again
Lifted. Then only the disembodied cry
Going with the human, while she runs in a circle
On the leash of the cry. While the wind
Presses outer space into the grass
And alarms wrens deep in brambles
With hissing fragments of stars.

# Tractor

The tractor stands frozen—an agony
To think of. All night
Snow packed its open entrails. Now a head-pincering gale,
A spill of molten ice, smoking snow,
Pours into its steel.
At white heat of numbness it stands
In the aimed hosing of ground-level fieriness.

It defies flesh and won't start.
Hands are like wounds already
Inside armor gloves, and feet are unbelievable
As if the toenails were all just torn off.
I stare at it in hatred. Beyond it
The copse hisses—capitulates miserably
In the fleeing, failing light. Starlings,
A dirtier sleetier snow, blow smokily, unendingly, over
Towards plantations eastward.
All the time the tractor is sinking
Through the degrees, deepening
Into its hell of ice.

The starting lever
Cracks its action, like a snapping knuckle.
The battery is alive—but like a lamb
Trying to nudge its solid-frozen mother—
While the seat claims my buttock-bones, bites
With the space-cold of earth, which it has joined
In one solid lump.

I squirt commercial sure-fire
Down the black throat—it just coughs.
It ridicules me—a trap of iron stupidity
I've stepped into. I drive the battery
As if I were hammering and hammering
The frozen arrangement to pieces with a hammer
And it jabbers laughing pain-crying mockingly
Into happy life.

And stands
Shuddering itself full of heat, seeming to enlarge slowly
Like a demon demonstrating
A more than usually complete materialization—
Suddenly it jerks from its solidarity
With the concrete, and lurches towards a stanchion
Bursting with superhuman well-being and abandon
Shouting Where? Where?

Worse iron is waiting. Power-lift kneels,
Levers awake imprisoned deadweight,
Shackle pins bedded in cast-iron cow shit.
The blind and vibrating condemned obedience
Of iron to the cruelty of iron,
Wheels screeched out of their night locks—

Fingers
Among the tormented
Tonnage and burning of iron

Eyes
Weeping in the wind of chloroform

And the tractor, streaming with sweat,
Raging and trembling and rejoicing.

# Roe Deer

In the dawn-dirty light, in the biggest snow of the year
Two blue-dark deer stood in the road, alerted.

They had happened into my dimension
The moment I was arriving just there.

They planted their two or three years of secret deerhood
Clear on my snow-screen vision of the abnormal

And hesitated in the all-way disintegration
And stared at me. And so for some lasting seconds

I could think the deer were waiting for me
To remember the password and sign

That the curtain had blown aside for a moment
And there where the trees were no longer trees, nor the road
                                                a road

The deer had come for me.

Then they ducked through the hedge, and upright they rode
                                                their legs
Away downhill over a snow-lonely field

Towards tree-dark—finally
Seeming to eddy and glide and fly away up

Into the boil of big flakes.
The snow took them and soon their nearby hoofprints as well

Revising its dawn inspiration
Back to the ordinary.

# Couples Under Cover

The ewes are in the shed
Under clapping wings of corrugated iron
Where entering rays of snow cut horizontal
Fiery and radioactive, a star dust.
The oaks outside, half digested
With a writhing white fire-snow off the hill-field
Burning to frails of charcoal,
Roar blind, and swing blindly, a hilltop
Helpless self-defense. Snow
Is erasing them, whitening blanks
Against a dirty whiteness. The new jolly lambs
Are pleased with their nursery. A few cavorts
Keep trying their hind legs—up and a twist,
So they stagger back to balance, bewildered
By the life that's working at them. Heads, safer,
Home in on udders, undergroin hot flesh tent,
Hide eyes in muggy snugness. The ewes can't settle,
Heads bony and ratty with anxiety,
Keyed to every wind shift, light-footed
To leap clear when the hilltop
Starts to peel off, or those tortured tree-oceans
Come blundering through the old stonework.
They don't appreciate the comfort.
They'd as soon be in midfield suffering
The twenty-mile snow gale of unprotection,
Ice balls anesthetizing their back-end blood tatters,
Watching and worrying while a lamb grows stranger—

A rumpy-humped skinned-looking rabbit
Whose hunger no longer works.

                              One day
Of slightly unnatural natural comfort, and the lambs
Will toss out into the snow, imperishable
Like trawlers, bobbing in gangs, while the world
Welters unconscious into whiteness.

# Surprise

Looking at cows in their high-roofy roomy
Windy home, midafternoon idling,
Late winter, near spring, the fields not greening,
The wind northeast and sickening, the hay
Shrinking, the year growing. The parapets
Of toppled hay, the broken walls of hay,
The debris of hay. The peace of cattle
Midafternoon, cud-munching, eyelids lowered.
The deep platform of dung. Looking at cows
Sharing their trance, it was an anomalous
Blue plastic apron I noticed
Hitched under the tail of one cow
That went on munching, with angling ears. A glistening
Hanging sheet of blue-black. I thought
Of aprons over ewes' back ends
To keep the ram out till it's timely. I thought
Of surgical aprons to keep cleanliness
Under the shit-fall. Crazily far thoughts
Proposed themselves as natural, and I almost
Looked away. Suddenly
The apron slithered, and a whole calf's
Buttocks and hind legs—whose head and forefeet
Had been hidden from me by another cow—
Toppled out of its mother, and collapsed on the ground.
Leisurely, as she might be leisurely curious,
She turned, pulling her streamers of blood-tissue
Away from this lumpish jetsam. She nosed it
Where it lay like a stillbirth in its tissues.

She began to nibble and lick. The jelly
Shook its head and nosed the air. She gave it
The short small swallowed moo-grunts hungry cows
Give when they stand suddenly among plenty.

# Last Night

She would not leave her dead twins. The whole flock
Went on into the next field, over the hill,
But she stayed with her corpses. We took one
And left one to keep her happy.
The north wind brought the worst cold
Of this winter. Before dawn
It shifted a little and wetter. First light, the mist
Was like a nail in the head. She had gone through
Into the next field, but still lingered
Within close crying of her lamb, who lay now
Without eyes, already entrails pulled out
Between his legs. She cried for him to follow,
Now she felt so much lighter. As she cried
The two rams came bobbing over the hill,
The grayface and the blackface.

                             They came straight on,
Noses stretching forward as if they were being pulled
By nose rings. They milled merrily round her,
Fitting their awkward bodies to the requirement
That was calling, and that they could not resist
Or properly understand yet. Confusion of smells
And excitements. She ran off. They followed.
The grayface squared back and bounced his brow
Off the head of the surprised blackface, who stopped.
The grayface hurried on and now she followed.
He was leading her away and she followed.
She had stopped crying to her silent lamb.
The blackface caught them up on the steepness.

The grayface shouldered her away, drew back
Six or seven paces, dragging his forelegs, then curling his head
He bounded forward and the other met him.
The blackface stood sideways. Then the grayface
Hurried to huddle with her. She hurried nibbling,
Making up for all she'd missed with her crying.
Then blackface came again. The two jostled her,
Both trying to mount her simultaneously
As she ran between them and under them
Hurrying to nibble further.
They drew back and bounced and collided again.
The grayface turned away as if
He'd done something quite slight but necessary
And mounted her as she nibbled. There he stayed.
The blackface ran at her and, baffled, paused.
Searched where to attack to get her for himself.
The grayface withdrew and flopped off,
And she ran on nibbling. The two rams
Turned to stare at me.
Two or three lambs wobbled in the cold.

# Ravens

As we came through the gate to look at the few new lambs
On the skyline of lawn smoothness,
A raven bundled itself into air from midfield
And slid away under hard glistenings, low and guilty.
Sheep nibbling, kneeling to nibble the reluctant nibbled grass.
Sheep staring, their jaws pausing to think, then chewing
                                                again,
Then pausing. Over there a new lamb
Just getting up, bumping its mother's nose
As she nibbles the sugar coating off it
While the tattered banners of her triumph swing and drip
                                        from her rear end.
She sneezes and a glim of water flashes from her rear end.
She sneezes again and again, till she's emptied.
She carries on investigating her new present and seeing how
                                                it works.
Over here is something else. But you are still interested
In that new one, and its new spark of voice,
And its tininess.
Now over here, where the raven was,
Is what interests you next. Born dead,
Twisted like a scarf, a lamb of an hour or two,
Its insides, the various jellies and crimsons and transparencies
And threads and tissues pulled out
In straight lines, like tent ropes
From its upward belly opened like a lamb-wool slipper,
The fine anatomy of silvery ribs on display and the cavity,
The head also emptied through the eye sockets,

The woolly limbs swathed in birth-yolk and impossible
To tell now which in all this field of quietly nibbling sheep
Was its mother. I explain
That it died being born. We should have been here, to help
                                                          it.
So it died being born. "And did it cry?" you cry.
I pick up the dangling greasy weight by the hooves soft as
                                                  dogs' pads
That had trodden only womb water
And its raven-drawn strings dangle and trail,
Its loose head joggles, and "Did it cry?" you cry again.
Its two-fingered feet splay in their skin between the pressures
Of my finger and thumb. And there is another,
Just born, all black, splaying its tripod, inching its new points
Towards its mother, and testing the note
It finds in its mouth. But you have eyes now
Only for the tattered bundle of throwaway lamb.
"Did it cry?" you keep asking, in a three-year-old field-wide
Piercing persistence. "Oh, yes," I say, "it cried,"

Though this one was lucky insofar
As it made the attempt into a warm wind
And its first day of death was blue and warm
The magpies gone quiet with domestic happiness
And skylarks not worrying about anything
And the blackthorn budding confidently
And the skyline of hills, after millions of hard years,
Sitting soft.

31

# February 17th

A lamb could not get born. Ice wind
Out of a downpour dishclout sunrise. The mother
Lay on the mudded slope. Harried, she got up
And the blackish lump bobbed at her back end
Under her tail. After some hard galloping,
Some maneuvering, much flapping of the backward
Lump head of the lamb looking out,
I caught her with a rope. Laid her, head uphill,
And examined the lamb. A blood ball swollen
Tight in its black felt, its mouth gap
Squashed crooked, tongue stuck out, black-purple,
Strangled by its mother. I felt inside,
Past the noose of mother-flesh, into the slippery
Muscled tunnel, fingering for a hoof,
Right back to the porthole of the pelvis.
But there was no hoof. He had stuck his head out too early
And his feet could not follow. He should have
Felt his way, tiptoe, his toes
Tucked up under his nose
For a safe landing. So I kneeled wrestling
With her groans. No hand could squeeze past
The lamb's neck into her interior
To hook a knee. I roped that baby head
And hauled till she cried out and tried
To get up and I saw it was useless. I went
Two miles for the injection and a razor.
Sliced the lamb's throat strings, levered with a knife
Between the vertebrae and brought the head off

To stare at its mother, its pipes sitting in the mud
With all earth for a body. Then pushed
The neck stump right back in, and as I pushed
She pushed. She pushed crying and I pushed gasping.
And the strength
Of the birth push and the push of my thumb
Against that wobbly vertebra were deadlock,
A to-fro futility. Till I forced
A hand past and got a knee. Then like
Pulling myself to the ceiling with one finger
Hooked in a loop, timing my effort
To her birth-push groans, I pulled against
The corpse that would not come. Till it came.
And after it the long, sudden, yolk-yellow
Parcel of life
In a smoking slither of oils and soups and syrups—
And the body lay born, beside the hacked-off head.

# March Morning Unlike Others

Blue haze. Bees hanging in air at the hive mouth.
Crawling in prone stupor of sun
On the hive lip. Snowdrops. Two buzzards,
Still-wings, each
Magnetized to the other,
Float orbits.
Cattle standing warm. Lit, happy stillness.
A raven, under the hill,
Coughing among bare oaks.
Aircraft, elated, splitting blue.
Leisure to stand. The knee-deep mud at the trough
Stiffening. Lambs freed to be foolish.

The earth invalid, dropsied, bruised, wheeled
Out into the sun,
After the frightful operation.
She lies back, wounds undressed to the sun,
To be healed,
Sheltered from the sneapy chill creeping north wind,
Leans back, eyes closed, exhausted, smiling
Into the sun. Perhaps dozing a little.
While we sit, and smile, and wait, and know
She is not going to die.

# Turning Out

Turned the cows out two days ago.
Mailed with dung, a rattling armor,
They lunged into the light,
Kneeling with writhing necks they
Demolished a hill of soil, honing and
Scouring their skulltops. They hurried
Their udders and their stateliness
Towards the new pasture. The calves lagged, lost,
Remembering only where they'd come from,
Where they'd been born and had mothers. Again
And again they galloped back to the empty pens,
Gazing and mooing and listening. Wearier, wearier—
Finally they'd be driven to their mothers,
Startling back at gates, nosing a nettle
As it might be a snake. Then
Finding their field of mothers and simple grass,
With eyes behind and sideways they ventured
Into the flings and headlong, breakthrough
Gallops towards freedom, high tails riding
The wonderful new rocking horse, and circling
Back to the reassuring udders, the flung
Sniffs and rough lickings. The comforting
Indifference and contentment, which
They settled to be part of.

# She Has Come to Pass

A whole day
Leaning on the sale-ring gates
Among the peninsula's living gargoyles,
The weathered visors
Of the laborers at earth's furnace
Of the soil's glow and the wind's flash,
Hearing the auctioneer's
Epic appraisal

Of some indigenous cattle, as if
This were the soul's timely masterpiece.
Comparing buttocks, anxious for birth dates,
Apportioning credit for the calf,
Finally climaxing her blood pressure
In a table-tennis to-fro strife

Of guineas by twenties for a bull
All of three quarters of a ton
Of peace and ability, not to say
Beauty, and to lose it, after all,
And to retire, relieved she had lost it, so,
As from a job well done.

# Birth of Rainbow

This morning blue vast clarity of March sky
But a blustery violence of air, and a soaked overnight
Newpainted look to the world. The wind coming
Off the snowed moor in the south, razorish,
Heavy-bladed and head-cutting, off snow-powdered ridges.
Flooded ruts shook. Hoof puddles flashed. A daisy
Mud-plastered unmixed its head from the mud.
The black and white cow, on the highest crest of the round
ridge,
Stood under the end of a rainbow,
Head down licking something, full in the painful wind
That the pouring haze of the rainbow ignored.
She was licking her gawky black calf
Collapsed wet-fresh from the womb, blinking his eyes
In the low morning dazzling washed sun.
Black, wet as a collie from a river, as she licked him,
Finding his smells, learning his particularity.
A flag of bloody tissue hung from her back end—
Spreading and shining, pink-fleshed and raw, it flapped and
coiled
In the unsparing wind. She positioned herself, uneasy
As we approached, nervous small footwork
On the hoof-ploughed drowned sod of the ruined field.
She made uneasy low noises, and her calf too
With his staring whites, mooed the full clear calf-note
Pure as woodwind, and tried to get up,
Tried to get his cantilever front legs
In operation, lifted his shoulders, hoisted to his knees,

Then hoisted his back end and lurched forward
On his knees and crumpling ankles, sliding in the mud
And collapsing plastered. She went on licking him.
She started eating the banner of thin raw flesh that
Spinnakered from her rear. We left her to it.
Blobbed antiseptic onto the sodden blood-dangle
Of his muddy birth cord, and left her
Inspecting the new smell. The whole southwest
Was black as nightfall.
Trailing squall-smokes hung over the moor, leaning
And whitening towards us, then the world blurred
And disappeared in forty-five-degree hail
And a gate-jerking blast. We got to cover.
Left to God the calf and his mother.

# Orf

Because his nose and face were one festering sore
That no treatment persuaded, month after month,
And his feet four sores, the same,
Which could only stand and no more,

Because his sickness was converting his growth
Simply to strengthening sickness
While his breath wheezed through a mask of flies
No stuff could rid him of

I shot the lamb.
I shot him while he was looking the other way.
I shot him between the ears.

He lay down.
His machinery adjusted itself
And his blood escaped, without loyalty.

But the lamb life in my care
Left him where he lay, and stood up in front of me

Asking to be banished,
Asking for permission to be extinct,
For permission to wait, at least,

Inside my head
In the radioactive space
From which the meteorite had removed his body.

# Happy Calf

Mother is worried, her low, short moos
Question what's going on. But her calf
Is quite happy, resting on his elbows,
With his wrists folded under, and his precious hind legs
Brought up beside him, his little hooves
Of hardly used yellow-soled black.
She looms up, to reassure him with heavy lickings.
He wishes she'd go away. He's meditating
Black as a mole and as velvety,
With a white face-mask, and a pink parting,
With black tear-patches, but long
Glamorous white eyelashes. A mild narrowing
Of his eyes, as he lies, testing each breath
For its peculiar flavor of being alive.
Such a pink muzzle, but a black dap
Where he just touched his mother's blackness
With a tentative sniff. He is all quiet
While his mother worries to and fro, grazes a little,
Then looks back, a shapely mass
Against the south sky and the low frieze of hills,
And moos questioning warning. He just stays,
Head slightly tilted, in the mild illness
Of being quite contented, and patient
With all the busyness inside him, the growing
Getting under way. The wind from the north
Marching the high silvery floor of clouds
Trembles the grass stalks near him. His head wobbles
Infinitesimally in the pulse of his life.

A buttercup leans on his velvet hip.
He folds his head back little by breathed little
Till it rests on his shoulder, his nose on his ankle,
And he sleeps. Only his ears stay awake.

# Coming Down Through Somerset

I flash-glimpsed in the headlights—the high moment
Of driving through England—a killed badger
Sprawled with helpless legs. Yet again
Maneuvered lane ends, retracked, waited
Out of decency for headlights to die,
Lifted by one warm hind leg in the world-night
A slain badger. August dust-heat. Beautiful,
Beautiful, warm, secret beast. Bedded him
Passenger, bleeding from the nose. Brought him close
Into my life. Now he lies on the beam
Torn from a great building. Beam waiting two years
To be built into new building. Summer coat
Not worth skinning off him. His skeleton—for the future.
Fangs, handsome concealed. Flies, drumming,
Bejewel his transit. Heat wave ushers him hourly
Towards his underworlds. A grim day of flies
And sunbathing. Get rid of that badger.
A night of shrunk rivers, glowing pastures,
Sea trout shouldering up through trickles. Then the sun again
Waking like a torn-out eye. How strangely
He stays on into the dawn—how quiet
The dark bear claws, the long frost-tipped guard hairs!
Get rid of that badger today.
And already the flies.
More passionate, bringing their friends. I don't want
To bury and waste him. Or skin him (it is too late).
Or hack off his head and boil it
To liberate his masterpiece skull. I want him

To stay as he is. Sooty gloss-throated,
With his perfect face. Paws so tired,
Power-body relegated. I want him
To stop time. His strength staying, bulky,
Blocking time. His rankness, his bristling wildness,
His thrillingly painted face.
A badger on my moment of life.
Not years ago, like the others, but now.
I stand
Watching his stillness, like an iron nail
Driven, flush to the head,
Into a yew post. Something
Has to stay.

# Little Red Twin

Sister of little black twin,
Is sick. Scour. Granny, their mother,
For a change from pampering the herd's growthiest bullock,
Has this year preferred a pretty pair

Of miniature sisters. But her power-milk
Has overdone this baby's digestion who now,
Wobbly-legged, lags behind the migrations
From field corner to corner. Her licked white face

Is still bravely calf-like, and does not
Comprehend the nonparticipation
Of her back legs, or that huge drag-magnet
Of reluctance to move. Oh, she is sick!

She squirts yellow soup and waits.
Blue Dartmoor waits. The oak by the trough
Swirls its heat-wave shadow-skirt so slowly
It's half a day's sleep. Little red twin

Has to get her body here and there
On only quarter power. Now, one eighth power.
Examiners conclude, solemn,
She might not make it. Scour

Has drained her. She parches, dry-nosed.
We force-feed her with medical powder mix.

We brim her with pints of glucose water.
Her eyes are just plum softness, they thought

She'd come to be a cow. Dark-lovely
Eyes to attract protection. White eyelashes
To fringe her beauty that bit more perfect—
They have to go along with her failing.

And now after a day in the upper eighties
There she lies dead. The disk harrow—
An intelligence test for perverse
Animal suicides—presented its puzzle,

And somehow she got her hind legs between bars
And fell as if cleverly forward, and locked
Where no mother could help her. There she lay
Up to eight hours, under the sun's weight.

As if to be sick-weak to the point of collapse
Had not been enough. Yet she's alive!

Extricated, slack as if limp dead,
But her eyes are watching. Her legs
Probably numb as dead. Her bleat
Worn to nothing. Just enough strength left

To keep her heart working, and her eye
Knowing and moist. Her mother

Had given her up and gone off. Now she comes back.
Clacks her ear tag, tack-tack, on her horn,

Watches in still close-up, while we
Pump more glucose water down her daughter's
Helpless glug-glug. Sundown polishes the hay.
Propped on her crumpled legs, her sunk fire

Only just in. Now some sacks across her,
To keep in the power of the glucose
Through night's bare-space leakage. The minutes
Will come one by one, with little draughts,

And feel at her, and feel her ears for warmth,
And reckon up her chances, all night
Without any comfort. We leave her
To her ancestors, who should have prepared her

For worse than this. The smell of the mown hay
Mixed by moonlight with driftings of honeysuckle
And dog roses and foxgloves, and all
The warmed spices of earth
In the safe casket of stars and velvet

Did bring her to morning. And now she will live.

# Teaching a Dumb Calf

She came in reluctant. The dark shed
Was too webby with reminiscences, none pleasant,
And she would not go in. She swung away,
Rolled her tug belly in the oily sway of her legs.
Deep and straw-foul the mud. Leakage green
From earlier occupants, fermenting. I tried
To lift her calf in ahead of her, a stocky red block,
And she pacific drove her head at me
Light-nimble as a fist, bullied me off,
And swung away, calling her picky-footed boy
And pulling for the open field, the far beeches
In their fly-green emerald leaf of a day.
We shooed and shouted her back, and I tried again
Pulling the calf from among her legs, but it collapsed
Its hind legs and lay doggo, in the abominable mud,
And her twisting hard head, heavier than a shoulder,
Butted me off. And again she swung away.
Then I picked her calf up bodily and went in.
Little piggy eyes, she followed me. Then I roped her,
And drew her to the head of the stall, tightened her
Hard to the oak pillar, with her nose in the hay rack,
And she choke-bellowed query comfort to herself.
He was trying to suck—but lacked the savvy.
He didn't get his nape down dipped enough,
Or his nose craning tongue upward enough
Under her tight hard bag of stiff teats each
The size of a Labrador's muzzle. They were too big.
He nuzzled slobbering at their fat sides

But couldn't bring one in. They were dripping,
And as he excited them they started squirting.
I fumbled one into his mouth—I had to hold it,
Stuffing its slippery muscle into his suction,
His rim-teeth and working tongue. He preferred
The edge of my milk-lathered hand, easier dimension,
But he got going finally, all his new
Machinery learning suddenly, and she stilled,
Mooing indignity, rolling her red rims,
Till the happy warm peace gathered them
Into its ancient statue.

# Last Load

Baled hay out in a field
Five miles from home. Barometer falling.
A muffler of still cloud padding the stillness.
The day after day of blue scorch up to yesterday,
The heavens of dazzling iron, that seemed unalterable,
Hard now to remember.

Now, tractor bounding along lanes, among echoes,
The trailer bouncing, all its iron shouting
Under sag-heavy leaves
That seem ready to drip with stillness.
Cheek in the air alert for the first speck.

You feel sure the rain's already started—
But for the tractor's din you'd hear it hushing
In all the leaves. But still not one drop
On your face or arm. You can't believe it.
Then hoicking bales, as if at a contest. Leaping
On and off the tractor as at a rodeo.

Hurling the bales higher. The loader on top
Dodging like a monkey. The fifth layer full
Then a teetering sixth. Then for a seventh
A row down the middle. And if a bale topples
You feel you've lost those seconds forever.
Then roping it all tight, like a hard loaf.

Then fast as you dare, watching the sky

And watching the load, and feeling the air darken
With wet electricity,
The load foaming through leaves, and wallowing
Like a tugboat meeting the open sea—
The tractor's front wheels rearing up, as you race,
And pawing the air. Then all hands
Pitching the bales off, in under a roof,
Anyhow, then back for the last load.

And now as you dash through the green light
You see between dark trees
On all the little emerald hills
The desperate loading, under the blue cloud.

Your sweat tracks through your dust, your shirt flaps chill,
And bales multiply out of each other
All down the shorn field ahead.
The faster you fling them up, the more there are of them—
Till suddenly the field's gray empty. It's finished.

And a tobacco reek breaks in your nostrils
As the rain begins
Softly and vertically silver, the whole sky softly
Falling into the stubble all round you.

The trees shake out their masses, joyful,
Drinking the downpour.

The hills pearled, the whole distance drinking
And the earth smell warm and thick as smoke

And you go, and over the whole land
Like singing heard across evening water
The tail loads are swaying towards their barns
Down the deep lanes.

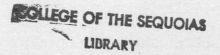

# While She Chews Sideways

He gently noses the high point of her rear end
Then lower and on each side of the tail,
Then flattens one ear, and gazes away, then decidedly turns,
wheels,
And moves in on the pink-eyed long-horned gray.
He sniffs the length of her spine, arching slightly
And shitting a tumble-thud shit as he does so.
Now he's testy.
He takes a push at the crazy Galloway with the laid-back ears.
Now strolling away from them all, his aim at the corner gate.
He is scratching himself on the fence, his vibration
Travels the length of the wire.
His barrel bulk is a bit ugly.
As bulls go he's no beauty.
His balls swing in their sock, one side idle.
His skin is utility white, shit-patched,
Pink-sinewed at the groin, and the dewlap nearly naked.
A feathery long permed bush of silky white tail—
It hangs straight like a bell rope
From the power-strake of his spine.
He eats steadily, not a cow in the field is open,
His gristly pinkish head, like a shaved bloodhound,
Jerking at the grass.
Overmuch muscle on the thighs, jerk-weight settling
Of each foot, as he eats forward.
His dangle tassel swings, his whole mind
Anchored to it and now dormant.
He's feeding disgustedly, impatiently, carelessly.

His nudity is a bit disgusting. Overmuscled
And a bit shameful, like an overdeveloped body-builder.
He has a juvenile look, a delinquent eye,
Very unlikable as he lifts his nostrils
And his upper lip, to test a newcomer.
Today none of that mooning around after cows,
That trundling obedience, like a trailer. None of the cows
Have any power today, and he's stopped looking.
He lays his head sideways, and worries the grass,
Keeping his intake steady.

# Sheep

## 1

The sheep has stopped crying.
All morning in her wire-mesh compound
On the lawn, she has been crying
For her vanished lamb. Yesterday they came.
Then her lamb could stand, in a fashion,
And make some tiptoe cringing steps.
Now he has disappeared.
He was only half the proper size.
And his cry was wrong. It was not
A dry little hard bleat, a baby cry
Over a flat tongue, it was human,
It was a despairing human smooth Oh!
Like no lamb I ever heard. Its hind legs
Cowered in under its lumped spine,
Its feeble hips leaned towards
Its shoulders for support. Its stubby
White wool pyramid head, on a tottery neck,
Had sad and defeated eyes, pinched, pathetic,
Too small, and it cried all the time
Oh! Oh! staggering towards
Its alert, baffled, stamping, storming mother
Who feared our intentions. He was too weak
To find her teats, or to nuzzle up in under,
He hadn't the gumption. He was fully
Occupied just standing, then shuffling

Towards where she'd removed to. She knew
He wasn't right, she couldn't
Make him out. Then his rough-curl legs,
So stoutly built, and hooved
With real quality tips,
Just got in the way, like a loose bundle
Of firewood he was cursed to manage,
Too heavy for him, lending sometimes
Some support, but no strength, no real help.
When we sat his mother on her tail, he mouthed her teat,
Slobbered a little, but after a minute
Lost aim and interest, his muzzle wandered,
He was managing a difficulty
Much more urgent and important. By evening
He could not stand. It was not
That he could not thrive, he was born
With everything but the will—
That can be deformed, just like a limb.
Death was more interesting to him.
Life could not get his attention.
So he died, with the yellow birth mucus
Still in his cardigan.
He did not survive a warm summer night.
Now his mother has started crying again.
The wind is oceanic in the elms
And the blossom is all set.

## 2

The mothers have come back
From the shearing, and behind the hedge
The woe of sheep is like a battlefield
In the evening, when the fighting is over,
And the cold begins, and the dew falls,
And bowed women move with water.
Mother Mother Mother the lambs
Are crying, and the mothers are crying.
Nothing can resist that probe, that cry
Of a lamb for its mother, or a ewe's crying
For its lamb. The lambs cannot find
Their mothers among those shorn strangers.
A half hour they have lamented,
Shaking their voices in desperation.
Bald brutal-voiced mothers braying out,
Flat-tongued lambs chopping off hopelessness.
Their hearts are in panic, their bodies
Are a mess of woe, woe they cry,
They mingle their trouble, a music
Of worse and worse distress, a worse entangling,
They hurry out little notes
With all their strength, cries searching this way and that.
The mothers force out sudden despair, blaaa!
On restless feet, with wild heads.

Their anguish goes on and on, in the June heat.
Only slowly their hurt dies, cry by cry,
As they fit themselves to what has happened.

# A Monument

Your burrowing, gasping struggle
In the knee-deep mud of the copse ditch
Where you cleared, with billhook and slasher,
A path for the wire, the boundary deterrent,
That memorable downpour last-ditch hand-to-hand battle
With the grip of the swamped blue clay, to and fro,
The wallowing weight of the wire roll,
Your raincoat in tatters, face fixed at full effort,
And the to-fro lurching under posts and tools and pile driver,
While the rain glittered all the sapling purple birches
And clothing deadened to sheet lead,
That appalling stubbornness of the plan, among thorns,
Will remain as a monument, hidden
Under tightening undergrowth
Deep under the roadside's car-glimpsed May beauty,
To be discovered by some future owner
As a wire tensed through impassable thicket,
A rusting limit, where cattle, pushing unlikely,
Query for two minutes, at most,
In their useful life.
And that is where I remember you,
Skull-raked with thorns, sodden, tireless,
Hauling bedded feet free, floundering away
To check alignments, returning, hammering the staple
Into the soaked stake oak, a careful tattoo
Precise to the tenth of an inch,
Under December downpour, midafternoon
Dark as twilight, using your life up.

# A Memory

Your bony white bowed back, in a singlet,
Powerful as a horse,
Bowed over an upturned sheep
Shearing under the east chill through-door draught
In the cave-dark barn, sweating and freezing—
Flame-crimson face, drum-guttural African curses
As you bundled the sheep
Like tying some oversize, overweight, spilling bale
Through its adjustments of position

The attached cigarette, bent at its glow,
Preserving its pride of ash
Through all your suddenly savage, suddenly gentle
Masterings of the animal

You were like a collier, a face worker
In a dark hole of obstacle
Heedless of your own surfaces
Inching by main strength into the solid hour,
Bald, arch-wrinkled, weathered dome bowed
Over your cigarette comfort

Till you stretched erect through a groan
Letting a peeled sheep leap free

Then nipped the bud of stub from your lips
And with glove-huge, grease-glistening carefulness
Lit another at it

# The Day He Died

Was the silkiest day of the young year,
The first reconnaissance of the real spring,
The first confidence of the sun.

That was yesterday. Last night, frost.
And as hard as any of all winter.
Mars and Saturn and the Moon dangling in a bunch
On the hard, littered sky.
Today is Valentine's Day.

Earth toast-crisp. The snowdrops battered.
Thrushes spluttering. Pigeons gingerly
Rubbing their voices together, in stinging cold.
Crows creaking, and clumsily
Cracking loose.

The bright fields look dazed.
Their expression is changed.
They have been somewhere awful
And come back without him.

The trustful cattle, with frost on their backs,
Waiting for hay, waiting for warmth,
Stand in a new emptiness.

From now on the land
Will have to manage without him.
But it hesitates, in this slow realization of light,

Childlike, too naked, in a frail sun,
With roots cut
And a great blank in its memory.

# Now You Have to Push

Your hands
Lumpish roots of earth cunning
So wrinkle-scarred, such tomes
Of what has been collecting centuries
At the bottom of so many lanes
Where roofs huddle smoking, and cattle
Trample the ripeness

Now you have to push your face
So tool-worn, so land-weathered,
This patch of ancient, familiar locale,
Your careful little mustache,
Your gangly long broad Masai figure
Which you decked so dapperly to dances,
Your hawser and lever strength
Which you used, so recklessly,
Like a tractor, guaranteed unbreakable

Now you have to push it all—
Just as you loved to push the piled live hedge boughs—
Into a gathering blaze

And as you loved to linger late into the twilight,
Coaxing the last knuckle embers,
Now you have to stay
Right on, into total darkness

# The Formal Auctioneer

Is trying to sell cattle. He is like a man
Walking noisily through a copse
Where nothing will be flushed. All eyes watch.
The weathered, rooty, bushy pile of faces,
A snaggle of faces
Like pulled-out and heaped-up old moots,
The natural root archives
Of mid-Devon's mud-lane annals,
Watch and hide inside themselves
Absorbing the figures like weather,
Or if they bid, bid invisibly, visit
The bidding like night foxes,
Slink in and out of bidding
As if they were no such fools
To be caught interested in anything.
Escaping a bidding with the secret
Celebration of a bargain, a straight gain
And that much now in hand.

When you were among them
Hidden in your own bidding, you stood tall,
A tree with two knot eyes, immovable,
A root among roots, without leaf,
Buying a bullock, with the eye gesture
Of a poker player
Deadpanning his hand. Deep-root weathering
The heat wave of a bargain.

# Hands

Your hands were strange—huge.
A farmer's joke: "Still got your bloody great hands!"
You used them with as little regard
As old iron tools—as if their creased, glossed, crocodile leather
Were nerveless, like an African's footsoles.

When the barbed wire tightening hum-rigid
Snapped and leaped through your grip
You flailed your fingers like a caned boy, and laughed:
"Barbarous wire!" then just ignored them
As the half-inch-deep, cross-hand rips dried.

And when your grasp nosed bullocks, prising their mouths
                                          wide,
So they dropped to their knees
I understood again
How the world of half-ton hooves, and horns,
And hides heedless as cedar boarding, comes to be
                                     manageable.

Hands more of a piece with your tractor
Than with their own nerves,
Having no more compunction than dung forks,
But suave as warm oil inside the wombs of ewes,
And monkey delicate

At that cigarette
Which glowed patiently through all your labors

Nursing the one in your lung
To such strength, it squeezed your strength to water
And stopped you.

Your hands lie folded, estranged from all they have done
And as they have never been, and startling—
So slender, so taper, so white,
Your mother's hands suddenly in your hands—
In a final strangeness of elegance.

# PROMETHEUS ON HIS CRAG

# 1

His voice felt out the way. "I am," he said

"Returning," he said, and "Now I am
Feeling into my body," and "Something is strange—

Something is altered." And he paused
Just within darkness, just within numbness.
He let his mouth-mask far off

Loll in the light.
"What has happened to me, what has altered?"
He whispered and he lay frightened—

Letting his veins venture for him
Feeling his ice-burned lungs gulp huge clarity
Letting his laborious chest lift him

Like the wingbeats of an eagle
                              and
                                   "Am I an eagle?"

# 2

Prometheus on His Crag

Relaxes
In the fact that it has happened.

The blue wedge through his breastbone, into the rock,
Unadjusted by vision or prayer—so.

His eyes, brainless police.
His brain, simple as an eye.

Nevertheless, now he exults—like an eagle

In the broadening vastness, the reddening dawn
Of the fact

That cannot be otherwise
And could not have been otherwise,

And never can be otherwise.

And now, for the first time
                              relaxing
                                        helpless

The Titan feels his strength.

# 3

Prometheus on His Crag

Pestered by birds roosting and defecating,
The chattering static of the wind-honed summit,
The clusterers to heaven, the sun-darkeners—

Shouted a world's end shout.
Then the swallow folded its barbs and fell,
The dove's bubble of fluorescence burst.

Nightingale and cuckoo
Plunged into padded forests where the woodpecker
Eyes bleached insane

Howled laughter into dead holes.
The birds became what birds have ever since been,
Scratching, probing, peering for a lost world—

A world of holy, happy notions shattered
By the shout
That brought Prometheus peace

And woke the vulture.

# 4

Prometheus on His Crag

Spotted the vulture coming out of the sun
The moment it edged clear of the world's edge.

There was nothing for him to do
As it splayed him open from breastbone to crotch
But peruse its feathers.

Black, bold and plain were those headline letters.
Do you want to know what they said?
Each one said the same:

"Today is a fresh start
Torn up by its roots
As I tear the liver from your body."

# 5

Prometheus on His Crag

Dreamed he had burst the sun's mass
And emerged mortal. He raised his earth-soaked head
Like a newborn calf. A skirl of cold air

Joggled the flowers.

And the exploded heavens peeled away
Into a mess of glare—the star-head rivets,
The hook-faced majesties of revelation

Writhed maelstrom-molten back
Into the heart's jar
That clapped again shut

On grasshopper silence.

                    He had resolved God
As a cow swallows its afterbirth.

But over the dark earth escaped
The infant's bottomless cry, the mother's lament,
The father's curse.

Prometheus on His Crag

Has bitten his prophetic tongue off.
Mountains gargoyle the earth
And the sea retches bile.

The thoughts that basted sweat down his flushed features
And carved his body in a freezing ecstasy
Like a last supper, are dead as Harakhty.

Heaven funnels its punishment
Into a heart that beats ostrich
Into a brain horoscoped cretaceous.

Below, among car bumpers and shopping baskets,
A monkey of voice, shuffling Tarot
For corpses and embryos, quotes Ecclesiastes

To the clock that talks backward.

# 7

Prometheus

Arrested halfway from heaven
And slung between heaven and earth

Swallowed what he had stolen.

Chains hungered. These chains were roots
Reaching from frozen earth.
They sank searching into his flesh
Interrogating the bones.

And the sun, plundered and furious,
Planted its vulture.

So the sun bloomed, as it drank him,
Earth purpled its crocus.

So he flowered
Flowers of a numb bliss, a forlorn freedom—

Groanings of the sun, sighs of the earth—

Gathered by withering men.

# 8

Prometheus on His Crag

Lay astonished all his preparations
For his humanity
Were disablements he lay disabled

He knew he could not walk he did not
Know how he could not crawl
He could not move he was a prisoner

Was he newborn was he wounded fatal
An invalid newborn healing
Bone fractures alert alarmed death numbness

Was this stone his grave this cradle
Nothingness nothingness over him over him
Whose mouth and eyes? A mother another

Prisoner a jailer? He spoke it was a scream

# 9

Now I know I never shall

Be let stir.
The man I fashioned and the god I fashioned
Dare not let me stir.

This leakage of cry, these face-ripples
Calculated for me—for mountain water
Dammed to powerless stillness.

What secret stays
Stilled under my stillness?
Not even I know.

Only he knows—that bird, that
Filthy-gleeful emissary and
The hieroglyph he makes of my entrails

Is all he tells.

# 10

Prometheus on His Crag

Began to admire the vulture
It knew what it was doing

It went on doing it
Swallowing not only his liver
But managing also to digest its guilt

And hang itself again just under the sun
Like a heavenly weighing scales
Balancing the gift of life

And the cost of the gift
Without a tremor—
As if both were nothing.

# 11

Prometheus on His Crag

Tried to recall his night's dream—

Where wrists and ankles were anchored, in safe harbor,
And two cosmic pythons, the Sea and the Sky,

Fought for the earth—a single jewel of power.
And the hammer-splayed head of the spike through his chest

Was a swallowtail butterfly, just trembling,

And neither wrist nor ankle must move—
And he dared hardly look at the butterfly,
Hardly dared breathe for the pain of joy

As it lasted and lasted—
                            a world
Where his liver healed to being his liver.

But now he woke to a world where the sun was the sun,
Iron iron,
            sea sea,
                    sky sky,
                            the vulture the vulture.

# 12

Prometheus on His Crag

Had begun to sing
A little before dawn
A song to his wounds.

The sun signaled him red through his closed eyelids
The vulture rustled
And the smolder of man rose from the cities.

But he went on singing—
A pure
Unfaltering morphine

Drugging the whole earth with bliss.

Prometheus on His Crag

Heard the cry of the wombs.
He had invented them.
Then stolen the holy fire, and hidden it in them.

It seemed to him
The wombs drummed like furnaces
And that men were being fed into the wombs.

And it seemed
Babies were being dragged crying pitifully
Out of the wombs.

And it seemed
That the vulture was the revenge of the wombs
To show him what it was like,

That his chains would last, and the vulture would awake him,
As long as there were wombs
Even if that were forever,

And that he had already invented too much.

# 14

Prometheus on His Crag

Sees the wind
Whip all things to whip all things
The light whips the water the water whips the light

And men and women are whipped
By invisible tongues
They claw and tear and labor forward

Or cower cornered under the whipping
They whip their animals and their engines
To get them from under the whips

They lift their faces and look all round
For their master and tormentor
When they collapse to curl inwards

They are like cut plants and blind
Already beyond pain or fear
Even the snails are whipped

The swifts too screaming to outstrip the whip
Even as if being were a whipping

Even the earth leaping

Like a great ungainly top

80

# 15

Prometheus on His Crag

Had such an advantageous prospect
He could see, even as he slept,
The eons revolving.

He could see, center of every eon,
Like the grit in its pearl,
Himself sealed on his rock.

Between the eons—dark nothing. But he could see
Himself wading escaping through dark nothing
From eon to eon, prophesying Freedom—

It was his soul's sleepwalking and he dreamed it.
Only waking when the vulture woke him
In a new eon
                to the old chains
                            and the old agony.

# 16

Prometheus on His Crag

Too far from his people to tell them
Suffers out his sentence
For having robbed earth of clay and heaven of
fire.

He yields his own entrails
A daily premium
To the winged Death in Life, to keep it from men.

He lays himself down in his chains
On the Mountain,
under Heaven
as THE PAYMENT

Too far from his people to tell them

Now they owe nothing.

# 17

No God—only wind on the flower.

No chains—only sinews, nerves, bones.

And no vulture—only a flame

A word

A bitten-out gobbet of sun

Buried behind the navel, unutterable.
The vital, immortal wound.

One nuclear syllable, bleeding silence.

# 18

The character neglected in this icon

Is not moon-head Io, or the hornet
That drove her through the limits.
It is not the vulture

With its solar digestion.
Is not even Epimetheus the twin
Who got away, in the end, with the heaven-sent girl.

Is not even the girl
With her gift pot, and its solitary hope.
Is not even the Almighty Presence

Of Everything.
The figure overlooked in this fable
Is the tiny trickle of lizard

Listening near the ear of Prometheus,
Whispering—at his each in-rip of breath,
Even as the vulture buried its head—

"Lucky, you are so lucky to be human!"

# 19

Prometheus on His Crag

Shouts and his words
Go off in every direction
Like birds

Like startled birds
They cry the way they fly away
Start up others which follow

For words are the birds of everything—
So soon
Everything is on the wing and gone

So speech starts hopefully to hold
Pieces of the wordy earth together
But pops to space-silence and space-cold

Emptied by words
Scattered and gone.
                    And the mouth shuts
Savagely on a mouthful

Of space-fright which makes the ears ring.

Prometheus on His Crag

Pondered the vulture. Was this bird
His unborn half-self, some hyena
Afterbirth, some lump of his mother?

Or was it his condemned human ballast—
His dying and his death, torn daily
From his immortality?

Or his blowtorch godhead
Puncturing those horrendous holes
In his human limits?

Was it his prophetic familiar?
The Knowledge, pebble-eyed,
Of the fates to be suffered in his image?

Was it the flapping, tattered hold—
The nothing door
Of his entry, draughting through him?

Or was it atomic law—
Was Life his transgression?
Was he the punished criminal aberration?

Was it the fire he had stolen?
Nowhere to go and now his pet,

And only him to feed on?

Or the supernatural spirit itself
That he had stolen from,
Now stealing from him the natural flesh?

Or was it the earth's enlightenment—
Was he an uninitiated infant
Mutilated towards alignment?

Or was it his anti-self—
The him-shaped vacuum
In unbeing, pulling to empty him?

Or was it, after all, the Helper
Coming again to pick at the crucial knot
Of all his bonds . . . ?

Image after image after image. As the vulture
Circled

Circled.

## 21

His mother covers her eyes.
The mountain splits its sweetness.
The blue fig splits its magma.

And the cry bulges.
And the veiny mire
Bubbles scalded.

The mountain is uttering
Blood and again blood.
Puddled, blotched newsprint.

With crocus evangels.
The mountain is flowering
A gleaming man.

And the cloudy bird
Tearing the shell
Midwifes the upfalling crib of flames.

And Prometheus eases free.
He sways to his stature.
And balances. And treads

On the dusty peacock film where the world floats.

# EARTH-NUMB

# Earth-Numb

Dawn—a smoldering fume of dry frost,
Sky-edge of red-hot iron.
Daffodils motionless—some fizzled out.
The birds—earth-brim simmering.
Sycamore buds unsticking—the leaf out-crumpling, purplish.

The pheasant cock's glare cry. Jupiter ruffling softly.

Hunting salmon. And hunted
And haunted by apparitions from tombs
Under the smoothing tons of dead element
In the river's black canyons.

The lure is a prayer. And my searching
Like the slow sun.
A prayer, like a flower opening.
A surgeon operating
On an open heart, with needles—

And bang! the river grabs at me

A mouth-flash, an electrocuting malice
Like a trap, trying to rip life off me—
And the river stiffens alive,
The black hole thumps, the whole river hauls
And I have one.

A piling voltage hums, jamming me stiff

Something terrified and terrifying
Gleam-surges to and fro through me
From the river to the sky, from the sky into the river

Uprooting dark bedrock, shatters it in air
Cartwheels across me, slices thudding through me
As if I were the current—

Till the fright flows all one way down the line

And a ghost grows solid, a hoverer,
A lizard green slither, banner heavy.

Then the wagging stone pebble head
Trying to think on shallows.

Then the steel specter of purples
From the forge of water
Gagging on emptiness

As the eyes of incredulity
Fix their death-exposure of the celandine and the cloud.

# That Girl

Promised by her looks, is saving up
To buy a maxi-coat.
It will not keep her warm.
She does not want
It to keep her warm. She wants it
To hurry her
Down that lane—which her wanted money
Conceals like a bank
Of flowers, and at the end of which,
When the flowers have gone,
She will lie naked on the bottommost weave of life
No better than a bacterium

But as joyful
And as coddled and supplied
By grateful nature
By young mother nature
By old father nature, too,
Hairy old man.

# Here Is the Cathedral

And here
Under the West Front saints' crumbling features
The Roman garrison bathhouse is being unearthed
Out of the dried blood of the redland marl—
Splayed, bleeding in rain, like an accident,
Gaped at, photographed, commented on, and coddled
With waterproofs. Nobody knows what to think of it.

And here are plague burials, incidentals
Surprised by the excavation—
Amber skeletons in their wedding chambers,
Touching couples, modest husbands and wives,
Dazzled awake by this sudden rude afterlife,
Cleaned with toothbrushes tenderly as hurt mouths,
Fleshless handbones folded over stomachs
Which no longer exist, and for faces
Clods of rained-on breccia—

And here
Under the tarmac brink, under headlamp chromes
Of Peugeots, Toyotas, Volkswagens, Jaguars, Saabs,
Spades have hacked an eight-foot vertical cliff
Through medieval solid bone-dump, skull-caps
Carried about by dogs, rib-struts, limb-strakes
Littering the redland mud, like trampled laths
At a demolition. And this is the House of the Dead,
Open to everybody.

                         And here is the door
Of the cathedral. Going in out of the rain
I met a dark figure in the doorway:

Shuffling on rotten feet in rotten shoes
The whuffling wino with simplified face,
Outsize R.A.F. greatcoat, trailing tatters,
Dragged lower by the black unlabeled bottle
In his pocket, was asking for something. A whimper.
A paw red as if sore, oily and creased,
Muffled some request.

                         Cash for renovations—
A cup of tea and a sandwich.

My first tenpenny piece conjured voices.
All my loose change shattered the heights—
And two furious ones, with sparkling faces,
With fierce heavenly eyes, with Sunday suits,
Arrived in a glare of question.

                         One swayed,
Crushing me with new worlds of consideration,
With angelic mouthfuls of sociology,
The other, pink-scrubbed, brass-eyed, Christian knight,
Was butting at the wino with his chest,
Impeccable godly fists clenched at his seams
At attention, like a police horse at a crowd,

He bumped the faceless mop of boy-black hair,
The dwarf-swollen nose, the coat on two shabby boots—

"How many times do you have to be told—out!
We've told you, haven't we? You do know, don't you?
Then out! Get out! Get out and stay out!"

Huddling mouse in his cloth,
Goblin aboriginal under his hair mop
Shuffled and tottered out.
                              Flushed with the work
Glistening righteousness and staring image
Wrathful commissionaires
Whisked back into the heights
Among columns and arches—

Leaving me an expendable tortoise
Of the war in Heaven.
                        Between masks
In rictus of sanctity, and the glossed slabs
Of the defunct.
                  With whispers
Draining down from the roots of the hair—OUT

OUT   OUT   OUT

# Postcard from Torquay

He gazed round, the tall young German at the jetty,
With a few words
That sounded like English so lordly
It was incomprehensible. It was actually *echt Deutsch.*

Under one hand, the uptilting stern of his glass yacht.
In the other, the dainty, quivering wind vane
Like a conductor's baton. He paused.
His two companions, almost English

In their woolly gloom, demoralized Bavarians,
Brother and bespectacled dull sister,
Hating England,
Humped by the brilliant yacht like too much baggage.

He narrowed heron-pale eyes
In the spanking midmorning Sunday wind
That bounced off the July sea, and panicked bunting
And slapped shots out of the stacked deck chairs.

He poised, in the wobbly mirror
Of the snapping puddles,
And the curl-mouthed glances of the rabble English,
Gazed over the sea's heroic bulge,

Then stalked off
In his minimal Continental sportswear,
Commandant—at home

On the first morning of Occupation—

To arrange, with lofty carrying words,
His costly yacht's descent
Into that swell of tourist effluent
And holiday turds.

# Old Age Gets Up

Stirs its ashes and embers, its burnt sticks

An eye powdered over, half melted and solid again
Ponders
Ideas that collapse
At the first touch of attention

The light at the window, so square and so same
So full-strong as ever, the window frame
A scaffold in space, for eyes to lean on

Supporting the body, shaped to its old work
Making small movements in gray air
Numbed from the blurred accident
Of having lived, the fatal, real injury
Under the amnesia

Something tries to save itself—searches
For defenses—but words evade
Like flies with their own notions

Old age slowly gets dressed
Heavily dosed with death's night
Sits on the bed's edge

Pulls its pieces together
Loosely tucks in its shirt

Pulls the clouds of star gas together

Leans on the doorframe, breathing heavily
Creaks toward the bathroom

# Nefertiti

Sits in the bar corner—being bought
Halves by the shouting, giggling, market-tipsy
Farmers who squabble to pay—

She hunches, to deepen
Her giddy cleavage and hang properly
The surrealist shocking masterpiece
Of her make-up.

She can't breathe a word
That wouldn't short out
The trip-wire menace
Of her precariously angled
Knees and wrist. Gorgeous, delicate,
Sipping insect,
With eyelids and lips
Machined to the millionth.

She gets her weird power
In the abattoir. All day you hear
The sheep wailing in religious terror,
The cattle collapsing to pour out
Their five gallons of blood onto concrete,
Pigs flinging their legs apart with screams

For the dividing steel
Of her pen in the office.

# A Motorbike

We had a motorbike all through the war
In an outhouse—thunder, flight, disruption
Cramped in rust, under washing, abashed, outclassed
By the Brens, the Bombs, the Bazookas elsewhere.

The war ended, the explosions stopped.
The men surrendered their weapons
And hung around limply.
Peace took them all prisoner.
They were herded into their home towns.
A horrible privation began
Of working a life up out of the avenues
And the holiday resorts and the dance halls.

Then the morning bus was as bad as any labor truck,
The foreman, the boss, as bad as the S.S.
And the ends of the street and the bends of the road
And the shallowness of the shops and the shallowness of the
                                                    beer
And the sameness of the next town
Were as bad as electrified barbed wire.
The shrunk-back war ached in their testicles
And England dwindled to the size of a dog track.

So there came this quiet young man
And he bought our motorbike for twelve pounds.
And he got it going, with difficulty.

He kicked it into life—it erupted
Out of the six year sleep, and he was delighted.

A week later, astride it, before dawn,
A misty frosty morning,
He escaped

Into a telegraph pole
On the long straight west of Swinton.

# Deaf School

The deaf children were monkey-nimble, fish-tremulous and
                    sudden.
Their faces were alert and simple
Like faces of little animals, small night lemurs caught in the
                    flashlight.
They lacked a dimension,
They lacked a subtle wavering aura of sound and responses to
                    sound.
The whole body was removed
From the vibration of air, they lived through the eyes,
The clear simple look, the instant full attention.
Their selves were not woven into a voice
Which was woven into a face
Hearing itself, its own public and audience,
An apparition in camouflage, an assertion in doubt—
Their selves were hidden, and their faces looked out of hiding.
What they spoke with was a machine,
A manipulation of fingers, a control panel of gestures
Out there in the alien space
Separated from them—

Their unused faces were simple lenses of watchfulness
Simple pools of earnest watchfulness

Their bodies were like their hands
Nimbler than bodies, like the hammers of a piano,
A puppet agility, a simple mechanical action
A blankness of hieroglyph

A stylized lettering
Spelling out approximate signals

While the self looked through, out of the face of simple
                                                    concealment,
A face not merely deaf, a face in darkness, a face unaware,
A face that was simply the front skin of the self, concealed and
                                                        separate.

# Photostomias*

## 1

Through roofless Gulf cellars
Hungers a galaxy.

Through black obsidian
A fossil ghost craves.

A feast, charged with lights,
Searching for guests.

Here is the radiant host.
Nobody loves him.

He is just what he looks like—a calculus
Woven by atoms on a lost warp of sunlight.

Quiet little Einstein
Of outer darkness.

His solution final—an illumination
Of fangs, a baleful perspective

Of the gravity
With which this universe shall consume itself.

At the sunken window of the world
He peers in.

*Photostomias is a small, predatory, luminous fish of the great deeps.

**2**

Volcanic, meteoric ooze
Opens an eye—lights up.
Apotheosis—Buddha-faced, the tiger
In his robe of flames.

                And no further
From belief's numb finger
Than the drab-jacketed
Glowworm beetle, in a spooky lane,
On a wet evening.

                The peacock butterfly, pulsing
On a September thistletop
Is just as surely a hole
In what was likely.

Star-hardened, over this scene,
The miserly heather flower, with his lamp,
Leans from the atom.

                Blossoms
Pushing from under blossoms—
From the one wound's
Depth of congealments and healing.

Earth is gulping the same
Opium as the heart.

**3**

Creation's hammer
Anvil of Nothing

A spark
A larval

Insect-frail
Gadget of spectrum hunger frenzy

A prisoner
A prison

Eros, dumbstruck, starving, staring
From a space-computer—

Glassy digits
Bottomless zero.

Jehovah—mucus and phosphorescence
In the camera's glare—

A decalogue
A rainbow

# Bride and Groom Lie Hidden
# for Three Days

She gives him his eyes, she found them
Among some rubble, among some beetles

He gives her her skin
He just seemed to pull it down out of the air and lay it over
                                                              her
She weeps with fearfulness and astonishment

She has found his hands for him, and fitted them freshly at the
                                                            wrists
They are amazed at themselves, they go feeling all over her

He has assembled her spine, he cleaned each piece carefully
And sets them in perfect order
A superhuman puzzle but he is inspired
She leans back twisting this way and that, using it and
                                        laughing incredulously

Now she has brought his feet, she is connecting them
So that his whole body lights up

And he has fashioned her new hips
With all fittings complete and with newly wound coils, all
                                              shiningly oiled
He is polishing every part,
                        he himself can hardly believe it

They keep taking each other to the sun, they find they can
easily
To test each new thing at each new step
And now she smooths over him the plates of his skull
So that the joints are invisible
And now he connects her throat, her breasts and the pit of
her stomach
With a single wire

She gives him his teeth, tying their roots to the centerpin of
his body
He sets the little circlets on her fingertips
She stitches his body here and there with steely purple silk
He oils the delicate cogs of her mouth
She inlays with deep-cut scrolls the nape of his neck
He sinks into place the inside of her thighs

So, gasping with joy, with cries of wonderment
Like two gods of mud
Sprawling in the dirt, but with infinite care

They bring each other to perfection.

# Second Birth

When he crept back, searching for
The womb doorway, remorseful, tearful,
It was an ugly grave
Fallen in on bleached sticks.
For flesh
It had dry bleached weeds over dry stones
Of a dried-up river.

Well it was a revelation to meet
Mother Death, a smack on the nose end
That inverted all his ideas.

There is nothing to be done
About what a head becomes
After years in wild earth.

And there is nowhere else to look for it.
And if what it says now
Can't be understood
Nothing else can speak for it.

Such words
Can only be swallowed, like stones,
And voided, or carried for life,
Or died of.

# Song of Longsight

No came from the earth
The egg Yes grew at No's nucleus
The egg hatched and No came out
Wet with Yes
And the voice of the No-bird was Yes

The No-bird reversed itself on a spike
Yes was now its ghost
Yes flew into a cliff-crack, like a rock-dove
So the No of Earth
Had to give birth and it was Yes

Yes was sick with No
Surgeons cut and found a star No
Which rose above earth, as her sign
A star like a sword, with downward point
Yes recovered

Living in uplooking fear and knowing
That whatever he begot on his kind
Could only be No
That whatever he conceived in his own heart
Could only be No
And there was nothing he could do or become
Which would not be No

The laws of space and matter are bitter

# Life Is Trying to Be Life

Death also is trying to be life.
Death is in the sperm like the ancient mariner
With his horrible tale.

Death mews in the blankets—is it a kitten?
It plays with dolls but cannot get interested.
It stares at the windowlight and cannot make it out.
It wears baby clothes and is patient.
It learns to talk, watching the others' mouths.
It laughs and shouts and listens to itself numbly.
It stares at people's faces
And sees their skin like a strange moon, and stares at the grass
In its position just as yesterday.
And stares at its fingers and hears: "Look at that child!"
Death is a changeling
Tortured by daisy chains and Sunday bells.
It is dragged about like a broken doll
By little girls playing at mothers and funerals.
Death only wants to be life. It cannot quite manage.

Weeping it is weeping to be life
As for a mother it cannot remember.

Death and Death and Death, it whispers
With eyes closed, trying to feel life

Like the shout in joy
Like the glare in lightning

That empties the lonely oak.

                        And that is the death
In the antlers of the Irish Elk. It is the death
In the cave-wife's needle of bone. Yet it still is not death—


Or in the shark's fang which is a monument
Of its lament
On a headland of life.

# A Citrine Glimpse

## 1

It was slender but

The chance flashed startling—a glance
A footfall

And stones leapt in their prison
Clay cried out in its chains
Bedrock, in its little case, cried with silent open
                                                    mouth

The sun watched through bars, stilled
Like one tortured too long
But the air
Wept for its long hopelessness and for joy
Water fell down where it labored
And worshipped full length, and leaped

He is alive
He who will free us all
He who will give us new limbs and eyes

It will not be much longer only days
He will lift us
We shall be in his arms, our fingers will touch the soul

And we shall enter the great beauty

We shall leap over each other, with him and his mate
Through the ecstasy flame

We shall sing through real mouths

For joy

The earth shook

## 2

He had hardly stepped

When he heard the water crying
He stared at it it continued to cry
And sob under naked shoulders

He stepped again
And the swamp quaked and a cry came
All the length of the reeds
A groan stifled and a silence worse

He stepped again
And stony words deep under his feet jabbered
He listened
As if he were empty sky listening

The stony words tore their throats and deepened on into a
hard agony
Beyond hearing, a silence that numbed

He stepped
And the moon in the bottom of the sea
Was a shriek, a gouging
The sea was like the hands and the hair
Of the moon
Whose shriek brought blood into the mouth
And was the dumbness of blood
And was the blackness of moonlight

Too late to flee
He hung
A nerve torn from the root of the tongue

The wind breathed on his rawness a word

And a wolf cried in its deformity

# Four Tales Told by an Idiot

## 1

I woke in the bed of the Rains

Of the fat sobbing one, the overflowing

Whose elephant madness
And rickets and dysentery and deprivation

Dropped on me like a krait
In a cellar of fruit machines

And held me in an amazon boggy fastness
Whose performance of misty bellowing

Acted the digesting a carven temple
In which I was the basalt stump of some god.

I escaped, in a malarial sweat,
To a worse chamber.

## 2

I was tied to a stake, in a tectite desert,
By lion-eyes

Who so focused the sun, with her glassy body,
She roasted my inmost marrow, my inmost ghost

Giving my skin no more than a slight flush.

Then she poured me water.

And so distorted the moon
She could grind my skull, not in the dimension of illusion,
With huge stones of illusion.

Then she gave me bread.

Then dragged the spinal cord out of me downward
Like a white-hot wire—

This she swallowed and became incandescent.

And lay down in front of me with my shadow.
The sun set, and they vanished together.


**3**

Night wind, a freedom
That wanted me, took me

Shook doors, and left shapes of me leaning there
Shook windows, which kept a faint print of me

Twitched gates, left a habit of me to squeak out in those
                                                    hinges
Shook trees, where twists of me still tangle

119

Swayed flowers, and much of me withered there later
Swept grass, the impress will not altogether release me

Stirred papers, wisps of me stayed snagged in hooked letters
Stirred garments, which motes of me will never be out of

Stirred river, which subtracted me from my reflection
Stirred fire, which shed me numb-frozen

On a cinder of heaven.


4

That star
Will blow your hand off

That star
Will scramble your brains and your nerves

That star
Will frazzle your skin off

That star
Will turn everybody yellow and stinking

That star
Will scorch everything dead fumed to its blueprint

That star
Will make the earth melt

That star . . . and so on.

And they surround us. And far into infinity.
These are the armies of the night.
There is no escape.
Not one of them is good, or friendly, or corruptible.

One chance remains: KEEP ON DIGGING THAT
HOLE

KEEP ON DIGGING AWAY AT THAT HOLE

# Actaeon

He looked at her but he could not see her face.
He could see her hair of course, it was a sort of furniture.
Like his own. He had paid for it.
He could see the useful gadgets of her hands. Which produced
food naturally.

And he could hear her voice
Which was a comfortable wallpaper.
You can get used to anything.
But he could not see her face.

He did not understand the great danger.

The jigsaw parts of her face, still loose in their box,
Began to spin.
Began to break out.
Openly they became zigzagging hounds.
Their hunger rang on the hills.
Soon they were out of control.

But the blank of his face
Just went on staring at her
Talking carpet talking hooverdust.

And just went on staring at her
As he was torn to pieces.
Those hounds tore him to pieces.
All the leaves and petals of his body were utterly scattered.

And still his face-blank went on
Staring, seeing nothing, feeling nothing

And still his voice went on, decorating the floor

Even though life had ceased.

# Seven Dungeon Songs

## 1   The wolf

Gazed down at the babe.
The beast's gangrenous breath
Clouded the tabula rasa.

The wolf was wounded in the jaw.
The blood dripped
Onto the babe's hands.
The babe reached towards the pretty creature,
Laughing a baby laugh,
A soft-brained laugh.

The wolf
Picked up the babe and ran among the stars.

The wolf's eye was icy with pain
And milk dripped from its tits.

The baby's cry
Echoed among the precipices.


## 2

Dead, she became space-earth
Broken to pieces.
Plants nursed her death, unearthed her goodness.

But her murderer, mad-innocent
Sucked at her offspring, reckless of blood,
Consecrating them in fire, muttering
It is good to be God.

He used familiar hands
Incriminating many,
And he borrowed mouths, leaving names
Being himself nothing

But a tiger's sigh, a wolf's music
A song on a lonely road

What it is
Risen out of mud, fallen from space
That stares through a face.


**3**

Face was necessary—I found face.
Hands—I found hands.

I found shoulders, I found legs
I found all bits and pieces.

We were me, and lay quiet.
I got us all of a piece, and we lay quiet.

We just lay.
Sunlight had prepared a wide place

And we lay there.
Air nursed us.

We recuperated.
While maggots blackened to seeds, and blood warmed its
stone.

Only still something
Stared at me and screamed

Stood over me, black across the sun,
And mourned me, and would not help me get up.


## 4

The earth locked out the light
Blocking the light, like a door locked.
But a crack of light

Between sky and earth was enough.
He called it earth's halo.

And the lizard spread of his fingers
Reached for it

He called it the leakage of air
Into this suffocation of earth

And the gills of his rib cage
Gulped to get more of it

His lips pressed to its coolness
Like an eye to a crack

He tasted the tears
Of the wind-shaken and weeping
Tree of light.


## 5

I walk
Unwind with activity of legs
The tangled ball
Which was once the orderly circuit of my body

Some night in the womb
All my veins and capillaries were taken out
By some evil will
And knotted in a great ball and stuffed back inside me

Now I rush to and fro
I try to attach a raw broken end
To some steady place, then back away

I look for people with clever fingers
Who might undo me

The horrible ball just comes
People's fingers snarl it worse

I hurl myself
To jerk out the knot
Or snap it

And come up short

So dangle and dance
The dance of unbeing


## 6

The oracle
Had nothing to say.

The crevasse
Was silent.

And the eyes of the witnesses,
The human eyes, jammed in flesh,
Which seemed to know, in their silence,
Were graves
Of silence.

And the tall rock of the sacred place,
An instrument, among stars,
Of the final music,
The final justice,
Was silent.

A bird cried out in the sky
As if the great crystal of silence
Suddenly split across.

But the rubbly dust at his feet
Could not utter
What it was humbled to.

And the great crystal of light
Healed, as before,
And was silent.


# 7

If mouth could open its cliff
If ear could unfold from this strata
If eyes could split their rock and peep out finally

If hands of mountain-fold
Could get a proper purchase
If feet of fossil could lift

If head of lakewater and weather
If body of horizon
If whole body and balancing head

If skin of grass could take messages
And do its job properly

If spine of earth-fetus
Could uncurl

If man-shadow out there moved to my moves

The speech that works air
Might speak me

# A Knock at the Door

You open the door
And you step back
From a sheltering bulk. A tumblesky wet January
Midmorning. Close, tall, inleaning
Hairiness of a creature, darkness of a person—

A bristling of wet-rotten woods, mold-neglect, night-weather,
A hurt wildness stands there for help
And is saying something. Wild lumpy coat,
Greasy face-folds and sly eyes and a bandit abruptness,
Speech nearly not speech
Ducking under speech, asking for money
As if not asking. Huge storm-sky strangeness

And desperation. He knows he stands
In a shatter of your expectations. He waits for you
To feel through to his being alive.
He wants to flee. His cornered wildness
Dodges about in his eyes
That try to hide inside themselves, and his head jerks up
Trying to fit back together odd bits of dignity,
And he goes on, muttering, nodding, signaling O.K., O.K.

Till you register: Money.

You give him bread, plastered with butter and piled with
                                                    marmalade,
And stand watching him cram it into his mouth—

His wet, red, agile mouth
In the swollen collapsed face.
His grimed forefinger cocked.

A black column of frayed coat, belted with string,
Has surfaced for help.
Stares into the house-depth past you
Stranger than a snow-covered starving stag.

Munches, wipes his fingers on his coat, and wipes his mouth
With the black-creased red palm.
A smile works his rubbery face
Like a hand working into a big glove.
His eyes wobble at you
Then an assault of launched eloquence
Like a sudden flooding of gratitude—
But you can't decode it.
He is extricating from his ponderous coat a topless bean can.
*Spot o tea in this ere, surr, if it's possible—*

A prayer to be invisible,
Eyes flickering towards the road as if casually
He dips his face to the scalding can's metal and sucks
Coolingly, hurriedly,
And now it comes again (the tossed-empty can back in his
pocket)
In a slither of thanks and salutes and shoulder-squarings
And sparring, feinting, dagger-stab glances

From the dissolved blue eyes
And the cornered mouse panic trying to slip into the house
past you—

MONEY.

Anesthetic for the big body,
Its glistening full veins, its pumping organs,
Its great nerves to the eyes,
Unmanageable parcel of baggy pain
With its dry-sore brains, its tied rawness—

You give him your pocketful and he buries it without a glance
And he's gone
Under his shoulder hunch, with hiding hands
And feet pretending no hurry
Under spattering and sneezing trees, over shining cobbles

To fall within two hundred yards
Dead-drunk in the church, to lie
Blowing, as if in post-operational shock,
Abandoned to space,
A lolling polyp of sweaty life, wrapped in its Guy Fawkes rags,
Bristling face-patch awry.

# Orts

## 1.   Each new moment my eyes

Open to the candidate
For being—
              but my brain closes
Exhausted, staled and appalled

But beyond that something opens
Arms
     like a host who has been
Watching the clock to the point
Of despair
          and like a swan launching
Into misty sunrise—

Convulsion of wings, snake-headed
Uncoilings, conflagration of waters

## 2.   Are they children

                 or are they senile?

A touch
And words scatter from him
Him, him and still more him
Like seeds
From Jumping Jack Balsam

And from the sealed, limestone, rockface lip
A drip

And  from  the  lightning-humped  oak,  out  of  its  lumpen
blazonry
Of burst mouths
Its gargoyle vaginas and old brain-wounds

A leaf—a leaf—a leaf


## 3.   For weights of blood

Granite farms.
For swaying breaths
Granite bridges.

For a watering eye
Granite walls
Granite headstones
For what is lost

For what adheres
To the lips' stir
As to the granite
A hand's shadow.

Granite oblations

Propped on the summit
For faceless presence
By soft-hand absence.


## 4.   Heatwave

Between Westminster and sunstruck St. Paul's
The desert has entered the flea's belly.

Like shut-eyed, half-submerged Nile bulls
The buildings tremble with breath.

The mirage of river is so real
Bodies drift in it, and human rubbish.

The main thing is the silence.
There are no charts for the silence.

Men can't penetrate it. Till sundown
Releases its leopard

Over the roofs, and women are suddenly
Everywhere, and the walker's bones

Melt in the coughing of great cats.

## 5.  In the M-5 restaurant

Our sad coats assemble at the counter

The tire face pasty
The neon of plaster flesh
With little inexplicable eyes
Holding a dish with two buns

Symbolic food
Eaten by symbolic faces
Symbolic eating movements

The road drumming in the wall, drumming in
the head

The road going nowhere and everywhere

My freedom evidently
Is to feed my life
Into a carburetor

Petroleum has burned away all
But a still-throbbing column
Of carbon monoxide and lead.

I attempt a firmer embodiment
With illusory coffee
And a gluey quasi pie.

## 6.  Poets

Crowd the horizons, poised, wings
Lifted in elation, vast
Armadas of illusion
Waiting for a puff.

Or they dawn, singing birds—all
Mating calls
Battle bluff
Crazy feathers.

Or disappear
Into the grass-blade atom—one flare
Annihilating the world
To the big-eyed, simple light that fled

When the first word lumped out of the flint.


## 7.  *Grosse Fuge*

Rouses in its cave
Under faint peaks of light

Flares abrupt at the sun's edge, dipping again
This side of the disk
Now coming low out of the glare

Coming under skylines
Under seas, under liquid corn
Snaking among poppies

Soft arrival pressing the roof of ghost
Creaking of old foundations
The ear cracking like a dry twig

Heavy craving weight
Of eyes on your nape
Unadjusted to world

Huge inching through hair, through veins
Tightening stealth of blood
Breath in the tunnel of spine

And the maneater
Opens its mouth and the music
Sinks its claw
Into your skull, a single note

Picks you up by the small of the back, weightless
Vaults into space, dangling your limbs

Devours you leisurely among litter of stars
Digests you into its horrible joy
This is the tiger of heaven

Hoists people out of their clothes

Leaves its dark track across the octaves.

## 8.   Lucretia

The buttercup lifts its wing cases
From between the claws
Of the retracting glacier.

Still it shakes out, on its crane stilt,
With its green core of tough subsistence,
Venturing over the bog.

So Lucretia has overtaken Englishness
The angler golden to the knees
The steeple at anchor on the river of honey

Just as she did the trekking weight of the mammoth
That jolted her cup
And set her pollens smoking.

## 9.   The cathedral

                    for all its defiance
Of the demolisher

Is ghost only.

As the coral island
Is the communal ghost of the corals.

As the jawbone
Goes on monumentally grinning
Over the spirit of temporal profit.

You too are a ghost—
The mountain, no less than the cat of the mountain—
Susceptible to a breath.

I too am a ghost
Where the airiest words

Move like ploughs,

             like bullets,

                  and like chains.

## 10.  Pan

Flowers open pits of allure.
The beast's glance makes the ghost faint.

Invitation in the bird's throat, a gobletful,
Wet mouth and hot undersoftness
Where the heart struggles at the surface.
Abandonment of water, long openings,
Disheveled silks, and nakedness of what resists nothing.

The painful stiff grace of insects
Making the stones ache.

So early earth, in stifled convulsion,
With bellowings, with gasps,
Roots torn up,
With life gushing from the body in relief
As eye widens against eye,
With death in hot bracken and birth under catkins

Yields her daughters.


## 11.  Speech out of shadow

Not your eyes, but what they disguise

Not your skin, with just that texture and light
But what uses it as cosmetic

Not your nose—to be or not to be beautiful
But what it is the spy for

Not your mouth, not your lips, not their adjustments
But the maker of the digestive tract

Not your breasts
Because they are diversion and deferment

Not your sexual parts, your proffered rewards
Which are in the nature of a flower
Technically treacherous

Not the webs of your voice, your poise, your tempo
Your drug of a million microsignals

But the purpose.

The unearthly stone in the sun.

The glare
Of the falcon, behind its hood

Tamed now
To its own mystifications

And the fingerings of men.

## 12.   Everything is waiting

The tree stilled in tree—swells in waiting.
The river stilled in flow—in away-flow push.

Even the birds, here and gone—
The sparrow hawk, bolt out of the oak tree
Slamming the crying dipper
Down through the water hatch

To hold its breath in bubble-cellar safety—

Are waiting.


## 13.   Night arrival of sea trout

Honeysuckle hanging her fangs.
Foxglove rearing her open belly.
Dogrose touching the membrane.

Through the dew's mist, the oak's mass
Comes plunging, tossing dark antlers.

Then a shattering
Of the river's hole, where something leaps out—

An upside-down, buried heaven
Snarls, moon-mouthed, and shivers.

Summer dripping stars, biting at the nape.
Lobworms coupling in saliva.
Earth singing under her breath.

And out in the hard corn a horned god
Running and leaping
With a bat in his drum.


## 14.   Flight from Egypt

He stole immortality
From the sleeping sun's disarray
Like moisture from the eye corner.

He stole beauty
From the sun's windy mirror.
He stole the laws
Like a hair from the beard of light.
He stole music
From the shell of the sun's ear.

He stole the cloak of joy
From the wall.

The slender daughter of the sun embraced him.

Together they fled, into darkness,
On the only beast available—

The ugliest of the ugly. And she fell off.


## 15.   Beeches, leafless

                         and lean hills
Muscle earth's grip on the core.

Cities, oceans, each thing anchors it
To the anchor of itself.

Yet it is weak. Weak

And unreal. Look—

                Dusk
Exorcises it, without effort.
And the whole globe flits, bat-like,

From this bright unaltered, unaltering place
Where you sit in final fear, and you,
And you still not daring to look up

Only waiting for me to touch you
And tell you again, "It's going to be O.K."


## 16.   Look back

See how he waves goodbye
Gingerly fathoming his own smile
See how he goes on waving

While the numbness grows in from his nails and hair
The ignorance from the platform and the soles of his shoes
The unknowing from the weave of his coat

The blindness from the bones of his face
The blindness of his skin
While the girdered deadness grows down from the station
dome

Till nothing is there
But his shape in its clothes
Noticed by nobody in particular

Walking tinily out of the station

# 17.   Buzz in the window

Buzz frantic
And prolonged. Fly down near the corner,
The cemetery den. A big bluefly
Is trying to drag a plough, too deep
In earth too stony, immovable. Then the fly
Buzzing its full revs forward, budges backward.
Clings. Deadlock.
The spider has gripped its anus. Slender talons
Test the blue armor gently, the head
Buried in the big game. He tugs
Tigerish, half the size of his prey. A pounding
Glory time for the spider. For the other
A darkening summary of some circumstances
In the window corner, with a dead bee,
Wing-petals, husks of insect-armor, a brambled
Glade of dusty web. It buzzes less
As the drug argues deeper and deeper.
In fluttery soundless tremors it tries to keep
A hold on the air. The north sky
Slides northward. The blossom is clinging
To its hopes, refurnishing the constant
Of ignorant life. The bluefly,
Without changing expression, only adjusting
Its leg stance, as if to more comfort,
Undergoes ultimate ghastliness. Finally agrees to it.
The spider tugs, retreating. The fly

Is going to let it do everything. Something is stuck.
The fly is fouled in web. Intelligence, the spider,
Comes round to look and patiently, joyfully,
Starts cutting the mesh. Frees it. Returns
To the haul—homeward in that exhausted ecstasy
The loaded hunters of the Pleistocene
Never recorded either.


## 18.  Lumb

At the bottom of the Arctic sea, they say.

Or "Terrible as an army with banners."

If I wait, I am a castle
Built with blocks of pain.

If I set out
A kayak stitched with pain.


## 19.  The express

                    with a bang
Lays its stationary blur
Of exploding stasis five seconds
Across our eyes where we loll

149

Blurred broader on benches.
It rivets ear holes, wind-tunnels
The world into a fleeing
Panic of atoms

Lifts the long trembling platform
To the dimension brink
Of disintegration. Wrenches
A whole dull covering off

Whips it away, claps it
Into its vanishing, amputated
Rear end, with a fireworks
Of blue and yellow, in under

Its black iron rockers . . .

                        That is how
You nearly arrived.

                    Already gone
Leaving silence mangled
And the flayed soul
Settling among steely gleams and cinders.

## 20.  TV off

He hears lithe trees and last leaves swatting the glass—

Staring into flames, through the grille of age
Like a late fish, face clothed with fungus,
Keeping its mouth upstream.

Remorseful for what nobody any longer suffers
Nostalgic for what he would not give twopence to see back
Hopeful for what he will not miss when it fails

Who lay a night and a day and a night and a day
Golden-haired, while his friend beside him
Attending a small hole in his brow
Ripened black.


## 21.  Ophiuchos

That face, real-skinned as iron
Those tears, like scars
Other faces also apply, with distortions

Hands reach spreading fingers
With barbed neighbor-raising screams

Body with raw mouth
The soul torn from the body

151

Cigarettes no working anesthetic
Careful kindness no tool in the tray
All sense the wrong shape and inflammable

Sleep horror waking worse horror

Only fire inexhaustible

Fining the marital metal


## 22.  Funeral

Twice a day
The brain-flaying ratchet of the storm cock
Announces the hawk here
With his implements.

Then for some minutes every bird in the neighborhood tolling
                                                    the alarm

Then a silence—
The odd starling crossing
Like a convict escaping,
The odd blackbird
Hurtling to better hiding, low.

And for the next half hour

A prison-state curfew execution silence, horrific.
Maybe a hedge sparrow weeping—peep, peep.

Somewhere the hawk's face patiently
Disentangles the fluff-belly
Yellow-gape, stub-tail throstling
From inside its pin-feathers.

But now, suddenly, the cool funeral bell.

Bill Fowkes, publican
Of the Ring O' Bells
Is meeting the King of the Dead.

Too deep in age and diabetes
For illusion,
With his gangrenous foot
He lay awake three weeks of nights
Hearing his black Great Dane announce him.

And at last he is being received—in person,
Bodily, irrecoverably
As if torn to pieces.

The leaves have a stunned, elated look.

## 23.   Children

                    new to the blood
Whose hot push has surpassed
The saber-tooth
Never doubt their rights of conquest.

Their voices, under the leaf-dazzle
An occupying army
A foreign tongue
Loud in their idleness and power.

Figures in the flaming of hell
A joy beyond good and evil
Breaking their toys.

Soon they'll sleep where they struck.
They'll leave behind
A man like a licked skull
A gravestone woman, their playthings.


## 24.   Prospero and Sycorax

She knows, like Ophelia,
The task has swallowed him.
She knows, like George's dragon,
Her screams have closed his helmet.

She knows, like Jocasta,
It is over.
He prefers
Blindness.

She knows, like Cordelia,
He is not himself now,
And what speaks through him must be discounted—
Though it will be the end of them both.

She knows, like God,
He has found
Something
Easier to live with—

His death, and her death.


## 25.   Before-dawn twilight, a sky dry as talc

The horizons
Bubbling with bird voices

The blackbird arrives a yard away, in a black terror
And explodes off
As if searching for a way out
Of a world it has just been flung into.

The shrews, that have never seen man, are whizzing everywhere.

Who is that tall lady walking on our lawn?

The star in the sky is safe.

The owl on the telegraph pole
Warm and dry and twice his right size
Scratches his ear.

Under the stones are the wood lice, your friends.

# Tiger Psalm

The tiger kills hungry. The machine guns
Talk, talk, talk across their Acropolis.
The tiger
Kills expertly, with anesthetic hand.
The machine guns
Carry on arguing in heaven
Where numbers have no ears, where there is no blood.
The tiger
Kills frugally, after close inspection of the map.
The machine guns shake their heads,
They go on chattering statistics.
The tiger kills by thunderbolt:
The god of his own salvation.
The machine guns
Proclaim the Absolute, according to Morse,
In a code of bangs and holes that makes men frown.
The tiger
Kills with beautiful colors in his face,
Like a flower painted on a banner.
The machine guns
Are not interested.
They laugh. They are not interested. They speak and
Their tongues burn soul blue, haloed with ashes,
Puncturing the illusion.
The tiger
Kills and licks its victim all over carefully.
The machine guns
Leave a crust of blood hanging on the nails

In an orchard of scrap iron.
The tiger
Kills
With the strength of five tigers, kills exalted.
The machine guns
Permit themselves a snigger. They eliminate the error
With a to-fro dialectic
And the point proved stop speaking.
The tiger
Kills like the fall of a cliff, one-sinewed with the earth,
Himalayas under eyelid, Ganges under fur—

Does not kill.

Does not kill. The tiger blesses with a fang.
The tiger does not kill but opens a path
Neither of Life nor of Death:
The tiger within the tiger:
The Tiger of the Earth.
                    O Tiger!
O Brother of the Viper!
                    O Beast in Blossom!

# The Stone

Has not yet been cut.
It is too heavy already
For consideration. Its edges
Are so super-real already
And at this distance
They cut real cuts in the unreal
Stuff of just thinking. So I leave it.
Somewhere it is.
Soon it will come.
I shall not carry it. With horrible life
It will transport its face, with sure strength,
To sit over mine, wherever I look,
Instead of hers.
It will even have across its brow
Her name.

Somewhere it is coming to the end
Of its million million years—
Which have worn her out.
It is coming to the beginning
Of her million million million years
Which will wear out it.

Because she will never move now
Till it is worn out.
She will not move now
Till everything is worn out.

# Stained Glass

## 1   The Virgin

Was silent.

She was so silent
The clock stopped, at a sheer brink.

So silent
The stars pressed in on her eardrum
Like children's noses at a window.

A silent
Carving in a never-trodden cavern.

So silent
The Creator woke, sweating fear

And saw her face stretching like a sphincter
Round a swelling cry.

Drop by drop

Like bodiless footsteps

Blood was collecting beneath her.

## 2   The womb

Ponders
In its dark tree

Like a crucifix, still empty—
Dreaming rituals of moon religions.

Dream after fruitless dream
Stains the feet of that tree
With salty drops of pain.

Between the fullness of its root
And the emptiness of its arms

It swells
A bud of hunger.

It blooms
A splitting sweetness.

It sings, through its flower
A silent lament

For the dark world
Hanging on its dark tree.

### 3   The Virgin Knight

How did she prepare?

What salt was her shield?
What lime was her spur?
What phosphorus her visor?

What sigh was her sword?
What strand of mucus her baldric?
What lust her charger?

What month's blood was her gauntlets?
What placenta her breastplate?
What sperm her helm?

What secret weapon, what *gae bulga*
Did she hide with a goatskin?

Her lance was her naked waist
Her oath—a wetness

Her battle cry
The silence between
Systole and diastole

Her heraldry a lily

And as she rode out

The hills quaked
The sea cried in fear
Incredulous
The stars trembled

# A God

Pain was pulled down over his eyes like a fool's hat.
They pressed electrodes of pain through the parietals.

He was helpless as a lamb
Which cannot be born
Whose head hangs under its mother's anus.

Pain was stabbed through his palm, at the crutch of the M,
Made of iron, from earth's core.
From that pain he hung,
As if he were being weighed.
The cleverness of his fingers availed him
As the bullock's hooves, in the offal bin,
Avail the severed head
Hanging from its galvanized hook.

Pain was hooked through his foot.
From that pain, too, he hung
As on display.
His patience had meaning only for him
Like the sanguine upside-down grin
Of a hanging half-pig.

There, hanging,
He accepted the pain through his ribs
Because he could no more escape it
Than the poulterer's hanging hare,
Hidden behind eyes growing concave,

Can escape
What has replaced its belly.

He could not understand what had happened

Or what he had become.

# ADAM AND THE SACRED NINE

# 1 · The song

Did not want the air
Or the distant sky

The song
Did not want the hill slope from which it echoed

Did not want the leaves
Through which its vibrations ran

Did not want the stones whose indifference
It nevertheless ruffled

Did not want the water

The song did not want its own mouth
Was careless of its own throat
Of the lungs and veins
From which it poured

The song made of joy
Searched, even like a lament

For what did not exist

Pouring out over the empty grave
Of what was not yet born

## 2  Adam

Lay defeated, low as water.

Too little lifted from mud
He dreamed the tower of light.

Of a piece with puddles
He dreamed flying echelons of steel.

Rigged only with twigs
He dreamed advancement of bulldozers and cranes.

Wrapped in peach skin and bruise
He dreamed the religion of the diamond body.

His dream played with him, like a giant tabby.
Like a bitten black-wet vole, even his morse had ceased.

Open as a leafless bush to wind and rain
He shook and he wept, he creaked and shivered.

# 3   And the Falcon came

The gunmetal feathers
Of would not be put aside, would not falter.

The wing knuckles
Of dividing the mountain, of hurling the world away behind
                                                    him.

With the bullet brow
Of burying himself headfirst and ahead
Of his delicate bones, into the target
Collision.

The talons
Of a first, last, single blow
Of grasping complete the crux of rays.

With the tooled bill
Of plucking out the ghost
And feeding it to his eye flame

Of stripping down the loose, hot flutter of earth
To its component parts
For the reconstitution of Falcon.

With the eye
Of explosion of Falcon.

# 4   The Skylark came

With its effort hooked to the sun, a swinging
ladder

With its song
A labor of its whole body
Thatching the sun with bird joy

To keep off the rains of weariness
The snows of extinction

With its labor
Of a useless excess, lifting what can only fall

With its crest
Which it intends to put on the sun

Which it meanwhile wears itself
So earth can be crested

With its song
Erected between dark and dark

The lark that lives and dies
In the service of its crest.

# 5   The Wild Duck

got up with a cry
Shook off her Arctic swaddling

Pitched from the tower of the North Wind
And came spanking across water

The Wild Duck, fracturing egg-zero,
Left her mother the snow in her shawl of stars
Abandoned her father the black wind in his beard of stars

Got up out of the ooze before dawn

Now hangs her whispering arrival
Between earth-glitter and heaven-glitter

Calling softly to the fixed lakes

As earth gets up in the frosty dark, at the back of the Pole
                                                    Star
And flies into dew
Through the precarious crack of light

Quacking Wake Wake

# 6　The Swift comes the swift

Casts aside the two-arm two-leg article—
The pain instrument
Flesh and soft entrails and nerves, and is off.

Hurls itself as if again beyond where it fell among roofs
Out through the lightning-split in the great oak of light

One wing below mineral limit
One wing above dream and number

Shears between life and death

Whiskery snarl-gape already gone ahead
The eyes in possession ahead

Screams guess its trajectory
Meteorite puncturing the veils of worlds

Whipcrack, the ear's glimpse
Is the smudge it leaves

Hunting the winged mote of death into the sun's retina
Picking the nymph of life
Off the mirror of the lake of atoms

Till the Swift
Who falls out of the blindness, swims up
From the molten, rejoins itself

Shadow to shadow—resumes proof, nests
Papery ashes
Of the uncontainable burning.

# 7 The unknown Wren

Hidden in Wren, sings only Wren. He sings
Worldproof Wren
In thunderlight, at wrestling daybreak. Wren unalterable
In the wind-buffed wood.

Wren is here, but nearly out of control—
A blur of throbbings—
Electrocution by the god of Wrens—
A battle frenzy, a transfiguration—

Wren is singing in the wet bush.
His song sings him, every feather is a tongue
He is a song-ball of tongues—
The head squatted back, the pin-beak stretching to swallow
the sky

And the wings quiver-lifting, as in death rapture
Every feather a wing beating
Wren is singing Wren—Wren of Wrens!
While his feet knot to a twig.

Imminent death only makes the wren more Wren-like
As harder sunlight, and realer earth light.
Wren reigns! Wren is in power!
Under his upstart tail.

And when Wren sleeps even the star-drape heavens are a
dream

Earth is just a bowl of ideas.

But now the lifted sun and the drenched woods rejoice with
trembling—

WREN OF WRENS!

# 8   And Owl

Floats. A masked soul listening for death.
Death listening for a soul.
Small mouths and their incriminations are suspended.
Only the center moves.

Constellations stand in awe. And the trees very still, the fields
                                                  very still
As the Owl becalms deeper
To stillness
Two eyes, fixed in the heart of heaven.

Nothing is neglected, in the Owl's stare.
The womb opens and the cry comes
And the shadow of the creature
Circumscribes its fate. And the Owl

Screams, again ripping the bandages off
Because of the shape of its throat, as if it were a torture
Because of the shape of its face, as if it were a prison
Because of the shape of its talons, as if they were inescapable.

Heaven screams. Earth screams. Heaven eats. Earth is eaten.

And earth eats and heaven is eaten.

# 9   The Dove came

Her breast big with rainbows
She was knocked down

The Dove came, her wings clapped lightning
That scattered like twigs
She was knocked down

The Dove came, her voice of thunder
A piling heaven of silver and violet
She was knocked down

She gave the flesh of her breast, and they ate her
She gave the milk of her blood, they drank her

The Dove came again, a sun-blinding

And ear could no longer hear

Mouth was a disemboweled bird
Where the tongue tried to stir like a heart

And the Dove alit
In the body of thorns.

Now deep in the dense body of thorns
A soft thunder
Nests her rainbows.

## 10   The Crow came to Adam

And lifted his eyelid
And whispered in his ear

Who has divined the Crow's love whisper?
Or the Crow's news?

Adam woke.

# 11   And the Phoenix has come

Its voice
Is the blade of the desert, a fighting of light
Its voice dangles glittering
In the soft valley of dew

Its voice flies flaming and dripping flame
Slowly across the dusty sky
Its voice burns in a rich heap
Of mountains that seem to melt

Its feathers shake from the eye
Its ashes smoke from the breath

Flesh trembles
The altar of its death and its birth

Where it descends
Where it offers itself up

And naked the newborn
Laughs in the blaze

## 12   The sole of a foot

Pressed to world-rock, flat
Warm

With its human map
Tough-skinned, for this meeting
Comfortable

The first acquaintance of the rock-surface
Since it was star-blaze,
The first host, greeting it, gladdened

With even, gentle squeeze
Grateful
To the rock, saying

I am no wing
To tread emptiness.
I was made

For you.